D0915711

Co-operation and Human Values

and Human Values

A Study of Moral Reasoning

Co-operation and Human Values

A Study of Moral Reasoning

R.E. Ewin
Senior Lecturer in Philosophy,
University of Western Australia

St. Martin's Press   New York

First published in 1981 in the United States by
ST. MARTIN'S PRESS INC.
175 Fifth Avenue, New York, NY 10010

© R.E. Ewin, 1981

Printed in Great Britain
First published in the United States of America in 1981

Library of Congress Card Catalog Number 81-526-11

ISBN 0-312-16956-6

Table of Contents

Preface

I shall be dealing, throughout this book, with a set of related problems: the relationship between morality and reasoning in general, the way in which moral reasoning is properly to be carried on, and why morality is not arbitrary. The solutions to these problems come out of the same train of argument.

Morality is not arbitrary, I shall argue, because the acceptance of certain qualities of character as virtues and the rejection of others as vices is forced on us by the co-operative basis of human life. The co-operation in human life is unavoidable; the alternative is a literal Hobbesian state of nature, and that is impossible. It is not that co-operation between people is a good thing or even a very good thing; it is simply unavoidable in human life, and it is impossible unless the qualities of character counted as virtues are encouraged and are at least fairly common. The possibility of human life presupposes a theory of human nature, and working out that theory of human nature is the main job of moral philosophy.

These virtues or qualities of character or attitudes lead us towards a theory of reasons. A person with a sense of justice is a person inclined to accept certain sorts of facts as reasons for acting, and if the virtues are presupposed by human life then the acceptance of those sorts of facts as reasons for acting is presupposed by human life. A condition of the life of reasoning beings (a more accurate term here than 'human beings') is that moral reasons are reasons for acting and are at the very basis of reasoning. And from this it follows that properly conducted moral reasoning is ultimately guided by the virtues rather than ultimately guided by a set of rules.

Moral rules have often been taken to have that ultimate role in moral philosophy. In my first chapter I shall show that that view is mistaken. In the next two chapters I shall show just what sorts of moral rules there are and what roles they do have, which involves giving an account of co-operation and an important way in which conventions can raise issues of justice.

1

That is followed by the beginnings of an account of justice. Chapter five deals with murder, which is, I shall argue, a species of injustice. It serves as an example of one way in which the concept of justice can be worked out in a detailed application, but also allows development of the earlier account by showing how, in the specific case of killing people, the possibility of human life presupposes, for the most part, the operation of a sense of justice in people. The first part of the major argument is then completed in chapter six. The argument shows that operation of a concept of justice as such, not merely in the specific form of a concept of murder, is presupposed by the possibility of human life, and is developed to show that acceptance of reasons of justice as compelling reasons for action is similarly presupposed by human life.

The other virtues are different. They are not necessary to human life as a sense of justice is, but, by their nature, make a co-operative human life easier. Reasons concerned with virtues other than justice are good reasons for acting, though not compelling. This is argued out in general terms in chapter seven. Chapter eight adds some flesh to the bare account of the other virtues by arguing out in more detail an account of kindness and its relation to justice, while more is added in chapter nine in an account of friendship, a moral phenomenon surprisingly often overlooked. With that, and with many interesting loose ends left, my argument comes to an end.

I do not, in this book, pursue all the issues in moral philosophy that my arguments raise. Still less do I pursue issues raised in areas outside moral philosophy, though they are frequently important and my arguments sometimes have implications for work being done in those areas. The main thesis that I pursue is clearly related to work being done in sociobiology, but, except for a couple of passing references, sociobiology is not mentioned. Part of my thesis has implications for political philosophy, especially about political obligation, but that problem is not pursued. An account of the virtues and vices plainly raises issues in philosophy of mind and the psychology of learning and moral development, but I have ignored most of these in my concentration on the relationships of the other virtues to justice and to reasons. That I have ignored these points does not mean that I consider them to be insignificant. It means only that I have restricted myself to one train of argument and have cut off a lot of interesting lines that might be pursued elsewhere.

Most of the work for this book was done in 1976 at Trent University, Ontario, during a year's study leave from the University of Western Australia, and could not have been done without that leave. I am grateful to the University of Western Australia for granting me leave, and to Trent University, especially Peter Robinson College, for providing me with facilities for my work.

The arguments in this book have been discussed with too many people for me to mention them all, though I always drew benefit from those discussions. Amongst my colleagues and students at the University of Western Australia I should particularly like to thank Julius Kovesi and Chris Ulyatt, and amongst those at Trent I should particularly like to thank Sandy McMullen and Jim MacAdam. I bear responsibility for all errors; none of the people mentioned agrees with very much of what I say.

Editorial advice from Professor Margaret Boden and Dr Terry Diffey did a lot to improve this book, for which I thank them.

I am very grateful to Lee Carter and Kath Shaw for their splendid work in typing from my untidy manuscript.

I am indebted to the Editors of *Mind* and *Philosophical Quarterly* for permission to use here, in somewhat re-written form, material which originally appeared in those journals.

Introduction

Hobbes was never perfectly clear about what it was that made man's natural condition into man's natural condition. He described it as a state of war of each against all, but descriptions in these all-or-nothing terms are plainly not essential; the outlaw is in his natural condition and may therefore be killed, but what will eventually control him is the combined power of those around him, who are not in their natural condition. The sovereign is described as remaining in his natural condition because he is not party to the contract. He may indeed be in a state of war with other sovereigns, but is no longer sovereign if he is in a state of war with the citizens amongst whom he usually lives. Hobbes also describes it as a condition in which all men have a right to all things, a state in which everybody is at liberty to do anything, and yet he allows that there could be some compacts. That surely entails the creation of rights in a sense inconsistent with everybody's being at liberty to do anything. In this case there may be further obscurity, because the claim that everybody is at liberty to do anything may be a substantive remark following from the claim that everybody is at liberty to do anything that he (honestly, possibly mistakenly, but without any chance of being over-ruled) judges to be proper.

Most of the conclusions that Hobbes wanted to reach, or conclusions very like them, can be reached from consideration of what would follow if there were no co-operation at all between people. Co-operation runs so constantly and so deep through our lives that it is easy to overlook it, and one point that should be stressed is that this imaginary state is one in which there is no co-operative way of resolving disputes, especially not for resolving clashes of interest (which people may or may not dispute). Consideration of this imaginary state throws light on the nature, structure, and basis of morality. It shows something of what continuing human life presupposes about human nature and organisation.

5

Whether I can be required to give you five dollars depends on the circumstances: whether I stole it from you; whether I borrowed it from you; whether I bought goods from you with promise of payment; whether my subscription to the Immanual Kant Fan Club is now due, and, if so, whether you are the treasurer; and so on. Whether I can be required to refrain from taking a picket off the nearest fence and striking you over the head with it similarly depends on the circumstances. It depends on whether you are attacking me with a view to taking my life when there is no chance for me to run away; it depends on whether you are attacking a little old lady and there is no other way to stop you; it depends on whether I can reasonably construe your presence as a threat because, even though I have never set eyes on you before, everybody I know hits everybody else over the head with fence-pickets unless forestalled, so that pre-emptive action is reasonable self-defence; and so on.

The point is not that whether I ought to meet requirements to give you money or refrain from hitting you over the head depends on whether it will pay me to do so; the point is that whether there is any such requirement for me to meet or fail to meet is dependent on the circumstances and, in particular, on how other people behave, have behaved, will behave, or might resonably be expected to behave. In man's natural condition, I shall argue, behaviour in general is such as to impose no requirements on anybody, so that it would be impossible to be unjust. Again, the claim is not that, in those circumstances, performing just acts does not pay. Acts which, in the circumstances in which we actually find ourselves, would be required by justice, are not so required in the circumstances of man's natural condition. In those circum-stances, no act counts as unjust. Equally, I shall argue, it is impossible to be kind in those circumstances. Acts which would be kind in the circumstances in which we now find ourselves would be, in the extreme circumstances of there being no co-operative relations at all between people, merely silly. Again, the claim is not that kindness would not pay in those circumstances, but that it would be impossible. Attempts at kindness would amount to silliness instead.

I shall argue, as these points suggest, that morality and a

social or communal life presuppose a background of co-operation for people and therefore presuppose, by and large, those qualities of character which are necessary for co-operation. Given that we have morality and a social or communal life, it is no accident that, by and large, people have, and encourage the development of, those qualities of character. In a slightly weaker way, it is no accident that, by and large, people have, and encourage the development of, those qualities of character which help in co-operation even if they are not necessary for it. Virtues are those qualities of character which are necessary for co-operation or which are, in the nature of the case, desirable in co-operation because they make co-operation easier and more efficient.

This does not mean that virtue-concepts are consequentialist concepts. *Repair* is a consequentialist concept: the test of whether something is repaired is, in rough and ready terms, whether it works again as a consequence of our tinkering with it. *Kindness* is not in that way a consequentialist concept: the test of whether an act was kind is not whether or not some co-operative enterprise works better because of it. The role of kindness in making co-operation easier explains why we should pay special attention to certain features of acts and count acts with those features as kind, but the role of kindness in making co-operation easier is not itself one of those features. Co-operative endeavour gives point or form to the concept of kindness, but is not part of its matter. Similarly, each of us may benefit from people's being just, and that may give a point to our being concerned about and grouping together those features that make an act just, but it is not itself one of the features and justice is not a self-interest concept. The organisation, or principle of organisation, of the features that make an act just cannot itself be one of those features or it could not serve its function.

Considerations in this vein provide us with a set of virtues that are in many ways closely related to Hobbes' laws of nature: peaceableness, trustworthiness, justice and so on. The same line of reasoning explains why morality, having the role it has in making communal life possible, is a matter of importance and not simply a matter in which we can properly choose our own code as we choose a brand of beer. It also explains the point with which I begin the argument: why morality is a matter of qualities of character rather than of rules, and why the role of rules in morality is much more restricted than is usually recognised.

It is no accident, I shall argue, that those qualities of character that are virtues are encouraged in the upbringing of children and other such activities. Those qualities of character involve tendencies to place importance on certain sorts of facts, so it is also no accident that we accept those sorts of facts as good reasons for acting. If rationality in any way presupposes social life, then it would be possible to show that reasons of justice provide overwhelmingly good reasons for acting and thus have a very special place in reasoning. In these terms I shall argue for the thesis, separate from my theses about the nature and structure of morality, that to be immoral is to act for reasons which the conditions of rationality show to be bad reasons.

The claim that there can be no morality or no social life without security is one thing; the claim that there can be no security without the sword to provide coercive backing is quite another. The first claim is true, the second false. Covenants without security are mere words, because covenanting requires amongst a group of people a whole institution or practice which is more than mere words; without security, we cannot covenant at all. The mere absence of a coercive sword, on the other hand, means no more than that covenants cannot be enforced in the face of determined infraction. Inability to enforce a covenant might be very important indeed in one case or another, but is quite different from the impossibility of making a covenant. Hobbes, unfortunately, ran the two separate claims together on his way to the conclusion that covenants without the sword are mere words.

Covenanting requires security because it is an inter-personal, co-operative practice. It requires a group of people who recognise mutual limitations, specifically by the rule that when, say, anybody signs his name to a document meeting certain specifications, he places himself under obligations set out in that document. Without that mutual recognition and the security that it constitutes, there can be no covenant.

Imagine a society in which nobody had ever covenanted, contracted, promised, or anything of the sort, and nobody had ever come across practices such as these in other societies, so that nobody understood what these practices were. When it comes to co-ordinating their activities so that one plants wheat while the other plants barley, or so that the felled tree does not land where somebody is standing, they have to make do with statements of intention as *we* understand that term. Nobody can undertake to do anything or place himself under an obligation; no matter what one has said about one's future activities, 'I changed my mind' is always a sufficient comment if one's actions vary from the stated plans.

Such a situation, in which nobody could undertake an obligation and commit himself to keep holding the ladder when the other had reached the top, would not allow people to arrange their affairs in a very efficient manner. Somebody pondering this problem when the ladder had fallen under him for the fifteenth time might hit upon the idea of promising or covenanting. Having done so, he might be able to persuade the others of the manifest advantages of such a practice. What he cannot do is introduce it on his own and leave others to follow his example. No matter how firmly he says 'I promise', he does not succeed in making a promise or giving to another person a special right if nobody else understands the word or the practice. Having said 'I promise to do X' he might set about doing X come hell or high water, and, should he nevertheless fail in his attempt to do X, he might make sure that he does something else to benefit the person who would have gained from his doing X and that he subjects himself to some unnecessary hardship as a spur to his resolve on future occasions. Nevertheless, he has failed to promise. His 'I promise' is simply an expression of great determination, a linguistic turn akin to saying 'I will' rather than 'I shall'. It does not succeed in transferring rights from him to anybody else.

Covenanting, contracting, promising, and so on, involve undertaking an obligation or giving over a right, and they do not thus transfer rights by magic. We co-operate with respect to these particular ways of being able to arrange our affairs, and, because we co-operate, justice gets a grip and obligations can be generated. They are enabling arrangements which make it possible for us to conduct our affairs more efficiently, and once they are in operation they generate obligations. We take a rule such as 'Once you say "I promise to do X" you must, in the absence of exceptional circumstances, do X', and we co-operate with respect to it, making claims on each other in the arrangements of our daily lives. It is a practice available to help all of us by opening up new possibilities, though the practice imposes no obligation on anybody to make use of the possibilities by making or accepting promises. When we do make use of it, though, we co-operate with others, calling on a general recognition of a limitation, *viz*. that after saying 'I promise' one does what one promised to do. If there is no co-operation, or no recognition of a mutal limitation, the obligation cannot be generated. It takes more than one person to co-operate, and it takes an agreed or accepted way of doing things. Covenanting, contracting, and promising require the security of co-operation in the form of knowledge that the other is co-operating. Whether this security can be gained only by holding a sword over the other person, or having somebody else to hold it over both of us, is a separate matter.

The role that co-operation plays in our lives is so fundamental that it is easy to overlook. We see the larger and more dispensable forms of co-operation, but miss the more basic ones. To cut travelling expenses, a group of people might co-operate by organising a car pool to and from work each day, and that might be convenient though unnecessary. On a larger scale, more people might each pay a levy which was used to supply a bus service. Two parents co-operate, agreeing, say, to get up on alternate nights with an insomniac child. These things we notice, but others we pass over. We co-operate if we resolve our dispute by going before an arbitrator, but we also co-operate if we simply discuss the dispute, recognising the mutual limitations imposed by justice, and sort things out for ourselves. As we co-operate in recognising the arbitrator and agreeing to accept his decision, so we co-operate in accepting the mutual limitations imposed by justice. In each case, we aim at some good, the resolution of the dispute, and we gain it by following a procedure that requires us to accept mutual limitations.

Any decision procedure other than that of a fight with the

spoils going to the victor is co-operative. There need not even be disputes: when interests clash, people often do not clash simply because they recognise the manifest injustice of pressing their interests in the given case; one reason that there are not many more diputes than there are is that most of us co-operate in accepting the mutual limitations imposed by justice, and we are so used to doing so that in most standard cases we need not even think about it. It is only when I search for odd examples that it occurs to me that, when I go home exhausted after a hard day sitting down in my office, I could serve my own interests and save myself cooking dinner if I simply went next door and stole my neighbour's meal. We co-operate in our recognition of the mutual limitations of a property system. Life is a lot more pleasant and a lot less violent because we co-operate in so many ways that we normally overlook.

Life would be very different indeed if there were no co-operation or if we could not, by and large, trust each other to recognise mutual limitations. In those circumstances, any clash of interests would mean a clash of people. Clashes of interest will be widespread when there is no settled way of life, so that I do not know where my next meal is coming from, where I may lay my head tonight, and so that each man who needs food threatens to make me wait a long time for my next meal. He would also make it impossible for me to care for my needs by growing grain or storing it, since, in the absence of co-operation, we could have no property system, and others would not only take the grain that I have grown but would do so with full right. Each man would pose a threat for me and I should pose a threat for each man; no one of us could lay his head anywhere at night with any security that others would not take advantage of his vulnerability while asleep and kill him to remove a threat. That, indeed, would be the sensible thing for them to do in those circumstances. Taking turns to sleep while others stand guard is ruled out because it is a form of co-operation.

In such condition, there is no place for Industry; because the fruit thereof is uncertain: and consequently no Culture of the Earth, no Navigation, nor use of the commodities that may be imported by Sea; no commodious Building; no Instruments of moving, and removing such things as require much force;

no Knowledge of the face of the Earth; no account of Time; no Arts; no Letters; and which is worst of all, continuall feare, and danger of violent death; and the life of man, solitary, poore, nasty, brutish, and short.[1]

The Hobbesian natural condition need not be predicated upon the nastiness of people. It can be understood as a thought-experiment about what life would be like if people did not or could not co-operate with each other. Because the removal of co-operation removes conventions, we might regard what comes out of this thought–experiment as an account of what people are like naturally, when free from conventions. But, even if it be true that people are, in that sense, naturally like that, it by no means follows that people are really like that. It might follow that it is impossible to have human life without conventions. The Hobbesian state of nature might be an impossibility.

The point is, indeed, stronger than Hobbes suggests, since he suggests that the matter would be merely one of great inconvenience. If we really take seriously such a state of nature, in which there are no conventions and no ways of resolving clashes of interest other than by fighting, and in which every person is a threat to every other person, then things follow that do not follow if we imagine instead very nasty people who live in the smallest possible groups, the members of each group co-operating with each other in the resolution of disputes that arise between them, but with the different groups constantly at war with each other. The latter may be more plausible as an account of what life was like before people had civil society, but, because it already involves social life and co-operation, a comparison of it with the present day does not reflect so well the role that co-operation plays in our moral lives. We must imagine a condition in which there is no co-operation at all and no resolution of disputes except by fighting, a condition in which all men are at liberty to do all things, and in which there is no property and no other individual liberty because there are no conventions to institute such rights and, in the absence of co-operation, nobody could take on the obligation necessary to give somebody such a right. In such a condition each man, and not merely each man's family, would be at war with everybody else.

In such a condition, no man could trust any other man or come to any arrangement with him. Life would be thoroughly solitary from birth to death. Unless one were raised by wolves, the period intervening between birth and death would be very short indeed. New-born babes cannot fend for themselves, and only a fool would limit his freedom and speed of movement by carrying around a child when he was surrounded by enemies, especially when the child would grow to be yet another enemy. Thus would the human race disappear within a generation of its appearance, and that is not the context in which we discuss and try to understand morality.

Beyond that, there is a question about whether such solitary creatures could have the language required for reasoning and could thus be people at all. Thought of the sort distinctive of rational beings (people, probably dolphins, possibly other beings) apparently requires an ability to use a language, some public form of communication. Some concepts, and especially those that mark off abstract thought or reasoning, can be possessed only by language-users. If words meant something different every time they were used then they would have no meanings at all, and we can tell that they have not thus subsided into gibberish only because we have checks on their constancy. Uncheckable constancy would not be sufficient; our *understanding* what was said is *our being able to tell* that the words have not turned into nonsense, not merely their not having done so.

We could not even have a Humpty-Dumpty sort of situation in which I knew what I meant even if nobody else did: how could I recognise my abstract thought apart from the possibility of expressing it and thus making it open to checks? Language serves us by performing certain tasks, and it can perform them only because it *could* fail to perform them; a signpost that does not guide me in some direction to the exclusion of others does not guide me anywhere.

Concepts, I think, are best considered as discriminatory abilities. The concept *red* discriminates some things from others, it can do so only because there are, or at least might be, things that are not red, and can do so only because it is possible to make a mistake in the discrimination which would have made a difference to something. The meanings of words

depend on the functions that they serve in our lives. We do not
form concepts arbitrarily, but because we need to make certain
discriminations, and the concept should be understood in the
light of that need, whether it be a need involved in the solving
of an abstruse mathematical problem or a need involved
simply in surviving in the everyday world. To understand the
concept, we must understand the point of discriminating in
that way.

The first value-word that most children learn is probably
the word 'dirty'. They learn it in learning to avoid certain sorts
of things, or in learning to have certain sorts of attitudes
towards certain sorts of facts. In the first instance, the child
may learn that he should not go round with jam all over his
face because it is dirty to do so. At that stage, if he thinks that
having jam all over the floor is unobjectionable, he still lacks a
satisfactory grasp of the concept of dirtiness. When he learns
that jam on the floor is dirty too, some sort of step has been
made, but he also needs to know that spreading jam on a slice
of bread is not dirty. Neither is putting floor wax on the floor
dirty, but putting it on bread is. Spitting on the floor is dirty,
too. Having earth or manure on one's hands while gardening
is not dirty, but going inside to eat a meal in that state would
be. The child's gaining the concept of dirtiness is not simply
his learning longer and longer lists of what is dirty and what is
not, but his coming to understand *why* things are classified in
that way. He must be able to extend the list himself and to
make judgments on new cases as they come before him.

His learning this is not merely a matter of his coming to see
certain empirical elements common and peculiar to all cases of
dirtiness, because even the short list already given makes it
clear that there are no such elements. Family resemblances
could no doubt be found linking the different cases of
dirtiness, but they will not do the job of marking off dirtiness
because family resemblances can also be found between cases
that are dirty and cases that are not: there is an obvious
resemblance between gardening with dirt on my hands and
eating with dirt on my hands, for instance. That resemblance
might not matter, but a family resemblance account of
concepts leaves us no way of explaining why it does not
matter.

Introduction 15

The reason for classifying in this way, then, is not found in empirical elements common to all cases or in family resemblances between them. Rather, it is found in human needs and interests. Briefly, people suffer from illness, illness is spread by germs, and germs breed in dirt. This classification answers to a human need to avoid incapacitation. People can grasp the concept of 'dirtiness', or the meaning of the word 'dirty', to greater or lesser degrees, but understanding it properly is moving towards recognising the function that the concept has in our lives. When we understand in this way, we know how to set about judging new cases that come before us. We can also see why some cases are borderline and puzzling, and we have an idea of how to set about resolving the puzzle because we know why certain properties are relevant to the dirtiness of whatever is in question. We see as well, in learning the word, why the fact that something is dirty is a reason for avoiding it.

Not all dirt causes disease, and not all causes of disease are dirt. Biological warfare may be dirty in one clear, analogical sense of the word, but it is not dirt. Spitting on the floor is dirty even if one follows the act by immediately dousing everything in sight with antiseptic. 'Dirty' is not shorthand for 'causes disease'. The concept 'dirty' is not a consequentialist concept at all. *Repair* is a consequentialist concept: what determines whether I have repaired something is whether, as a consequence of my tinkering with it, it works. What determines whether my face is dirty is not whether it causes disease. Disease gives a point to the classification *dirty*, but is not itself that classification. It explains why certain elements count as making something dirty, but is not itself one of those elements. Beyond that, the concept ranges in fairly obvious ways. Some things are dirty because they look dirty. Spitting on the floor is dirty, so we have reason for avoiding it rather than for creating more unnecessary work with a bottle of antiseptic. 'Dirty' is not equivalent to 'causes disease', but we can understand the notion *dirty* (let alone such notions as *clean dirt*) only if we see it in the context of disease and the role played by disease in human wants and needs.

This point does not hold only for dirtiness, nor just for value concepts. The sorts of considerations that I have, sketchily, brought to bear on dirtiness will apply to any concept. The meaning of a word, or the way in which it classifies items, properties, relations between statements, or whatever, depends on the function that it serves in our lives, answering to needs and interests, and the check on the constancy of its meaning is whether it keeps on serving that function. If it does, then life, or that particular part of it, goes on. Provided a particular lamp in the traffic lights looks red to us and therefore succeeds in regulating the traffic properly, it does not matter if the lamp has, if we can make sense of it, actually changed its colour. And we could make sense of that only if redness ceased to have some of the other significance it has in our lives; if, for example, an electric coil that looked the same colour as the lamp did not burn a hand that touched it, but one that looked green did.

Because words serve functions in our lives, there is a check on the constancy of their meaning and their proper use. Sometimes the check takes the form of an immediate brush with the physical world: if I start to misclassify in terms of colours, then I am likely to crash at an intersection. In cases other than those of present particular objects of sense, though, the only check that we can have requires language and communication with other people. The primary check then is agreement of judgments enabling us to get on efficiently with what we are doing.

Even reference to the facts as a check requires language. A red chair can be picked out from the rest of the world by lifting it with one's hands, but one cannot similarly physically separate the fact that the chair is red from the fact that the chair has a certain size or shape or weight. That sort of dividing up of the world is a conceptual task, and it requires the publicity of agreement in judgments about what is red which is necessary if redness is to serve the function in our lives that gives it sense.

This is more obviously so in the case of concepts such as *valid, follows from, possible*, and others involved in abstract thinking and reasoning. These can be expressed and checked only in a language, and, more important, they deal with essentially linguistic items. A statement may not be the same as a sentence, but one cannot satisfactorily explain what a statement is without reference to the working utterance of a sentence. The requirement for publicity in agreement of judgments will, therefore, come up at two levels with such concepts.

This sort of connection between language and reasoning and between language and publicity has often been argued, but it is not necessary for the position I shall defend in the body of this work. I shall later argue directly that reasoning requires a background of publicity and inter-personality.

The Hobbesian state of nature taken seriously, in which unsocial people live completely individual and unco-operating lives, is, therefore, impossible as an historical state for rational beings. In seeing why it is, we see what social life and morality presuppose about human nature, or one way in which moral philosophy is grounded in philosophical psychology. People must, by and large, be willing to co-operate with each other if there is to be social life, and, if reasoning presupposes the conditions of social life, people must be willing to co-operate with each other if they are to live as people or as rational beings. If, as I shall argue, willingness to co-operate requires a sense of justice, then human or social life presupposes a sense of justice.

Hobbes sets out his laws of nature as rules that people must follow in order to leave behind them their natural condition, but if we say that people could never have lived in that natural condition then we might re-read the laws of nature as a description of qualities of character that people must have, by and large, if social life is to be possible. A reasonable degree of peaceableness and trustworthiness are presupposed. We have, therefore, reason to believe that people by and large are relatively peaceable and trustworthy and that these qualities of character are social virtues. It will be no accident, whether it be a matter of heredity or of environment, that these qualities of character are fairly common and that facts concerning them are accepted as reasons for acting. Peaceableness and trustworthiness are not, of course, universal; the wars that we have throughout the world are sufficient testimony to that fact; but they are also a far cry from constituting a Hobbesian war of each against all.

So my argument leads to the conclusion that, in the context

of human life, it is no accident that certain qualities of character are encouraged and regarded as virtues and other qualities of character are discouraged and regarded as vices. It also leads to the separate conclusion that this fact gives moral reasons a special place amongst reasons in general. In each case, my argument is that the claim is presupposed by the possibility of social or human life.

If social life requires co-operation and co-operation requires a sense of justice, then justice will be the primary virtue. It is a basic condition of any social life at all. And justice, I shall stress, is a concept of reciprocity. The claim is not that it is not worth my while to be just if other people are nasty, but that other people's being nasty affects what justice requires of me; it is not, for example, unjust for me to fail to fulfil my side of a contract if the other party does not fulfil his. Other virtue-concepts are not, in that way, reciprocity-concepts, though they presuppose a background of co-operation if they are to have point. A sense of justice is the virtue that is necessary for social life, while the other virtues make social life easier and more pleasant. The parallel conclusion in the argument about reasons is that reasons of justice are rationally over-riding, and reasons of kindness, courage, and so on, are always good reasons.

NOTES

1   Molesworth (ed.), *The English Works of Thomas Hobbes* (John Bohr, London, 1839-45), Vol.III, p.113.

ONE
Abortion, roller-skates, and moral rules

Imagine it to be the case that there is a bye-law against taking a vehicle into the park. In the relevant book of rules it is written down for all to see: 'No.1: Nobody may take a vehicle into the park.' It is well-known that the bye-law is in force, and widely agreed that it is a good thing. After all, if cars were allowed into the park they would make tyre-marks on the lawn and knock down flowers, fast-moving objects might result in injury to the little children playing in the park, noisy traffic might upset the patients in the hospital across the road, and, anyway, it is nice to have a little bit of non-industrial greenery amidst the bricks just to remind us of what the country is like. All these points were made during the Council Meeting at which the bye-law was introduced, and one Councillor even added that he knew from private conversations that he was not alone in believing that the possibility of raising always-needed revenue from fines was a good reason for introducing the rule; since he was run down and killed by a car as he left the meeting, nobody ever did find out whether he was being facetious. Because of the widespread agreement with the enactment, infractions were few and far between. For a long time, only two charges were laid under the bye-law. One charge was against a man who drove a double-decker bus through the park; he was duly found guilty and sentenced. The other charge was against a ten-year-old who rode his broomstick horse through the park; that case was thrown out of court. When a third case finally turned up, it produced argument of interest.

One Sunday afternoon after watching the World Roller-Skating Championships, Mr Jones enjoyed himself by riding around the park on roller-skates and was duly charged by a zealous constable. At no stage in the court proceedings was it contested that a bye-law prohibited the taking of vehicles into the park or that Mr Jones had ridden through the park on roller-skates; the argument was devoted to the problem of

19

whether a pair of roller-skates constituted a vehicle. Various points were considered: the roller-skates were well oiled, and Mr Jones had not bothered the hospital; nor had he made any marks on the lawn, but he had knocked over some flowers and given a fright to some nervous children. Nobody questioned the existence of the bye-law, and nobody was under any misapprehension as to what Mr Jones had done; the argument was about whether a pair of roller-skates constitutes a vehicle, or whether the bye-law applied in this case, and that problem cannot be solved simply by invoking a law. Rules, ultimately, cannot be needed for the interpretation of rules else we should be faced with a vicious regress making the interpretation of any rule impossible. The argument is a typical legal one that cannot be settled by invoking the relevant law because it is about the interpretation of that law.

One can imagine a moral case presenting the same sort of problems. Consider, for example, the case of abortion. We might all agree that there is a moral rule proscribing the taking of human life (or some sophistication on that theme), and we might have a complete physical description of the foetus. Despite these two points we might disagree, as people who disagree about the legislation or the morality of abortion often do, about whether or not a foetus is a human being. This disagreement has the same form as that in the legal case above; it is a disagreement about the scope or interpretation of a rule, and cannot be settled by invoking the rule. I take it as plain that the disagreement about abortion can be a moral disagreement, i.e. it can be a disagreement about whether abortion is morally permissible or not. Similarly, the decision whether or not to abort can be a moral decision. Such cases are inexplicable in accounts of morality which place moral rules at the pinnacle, and claim that moral judgments must be justified by a process of deduction from moral rules and that moral decisions must be reached by means of practical syllogisms which have moral rules as their major premises. The rule will not do the job in the case of abortion, and, until such cases are argued away, Moral Rule theories of morality cannot be accepted as satisfactory. Moral problems typically do not have the form of a question such as 'Is murder wrong?', but rather the form of one such as 'When Othello killed Desdemona, was that

murder?'. They are, typically, questions about whether
something is an instance coming under a particular moral
concept. In some cases, such as that of a man who kills people
simply because they block his path to a partnership in the firm,
the answer will be obvious; in others, such as the case of
Dudley and Stephens[1], in which men shipwrecked on a raft
with little prospect of rescue agreed to kill the weakest of the
group (who never agreed to the idea) in order to provide food
and give themselves a better chance of survival, the answer
may be far from obvious.

I should like to make it plain that my concern is primarily
with the role that moral rules have commonly had in recent
moral philosophy[2] and not with their role in morality, though
it seems clear that a false philosophy of moral rules can lead to
distortions and bad judgments in moral life when, say, the
so-called man of principle insists on sticking to a rule rather
than concerning himself with the people and the particular
circumstances amidst which he acts. That there are moral rules
I readily agree; it is, by and large, not a good thing to swing a
sabre in a crowded room. It is equally clear that there are
people who are morally lost if they cannot find a rule to fit the
situation in which they find themselves; moral problems are
sometimes very complex, and having a rule to act at least as
some sort of guide can be a great help. What I object to are the
ideas that morality can be accounted for exhaustively in terms
of rules and that all moral justifications depend on moral rules,
or that morality consists ultimately of rules rather than of
ideals, virtues, notions, or what have you.

Having described a case of moral argument and drawn
conclusions from it, I shall devote the rest of this section to
consideration of some possible objections to my claims. The
first objection to deal with in order to make plain what I
suppose the scope of my argument to be is that the argument
would simply show, if it showed anything, that there cannot
be rules of any sort because problems of interpretation can
arise with any rule. The argument certainly does not show
that, and is not intended to; it is an argument specifically about
hard cases and is intended to show only that rules cannot be all
that there is.

When the double-decker bus was driven through the park,

then, clearly, the law was broken, and if I deliberately poison my wife to avoid disputes about property settlement in a divorce action then I break the rule proscribing the taking of human life. There is no problem about those cases. They clearly come under the relevant rules, and applying the relevant rules to get the answer that something illegal or immoral has been done is a straightforward business. Cases such as those concerning the roller-skates or abortion, though, are different because of the difficulties they raise. In such cases there are problems of interpretation which cannot be settled by invoking the rule because they are about the rule and its scope.

To repeat a point already made, I do not deny that there are moral rules and that they are in fact employed in moral reasoning; I deny only that moral rules do the full-blooded job that many recent philosophers have taken them to do, that of explaining and underpinning all of morality and moral reasoning. In some, though not all, cases, reference to a moral rule is not sufficient to settle the matter and is not really to the point, because the interpretation of the rule itself is what is in dispute. Faced with a question about the permissibility of abortion I shall probably find myself forced to reflect on the question of whether a foetus is a person. It will help by keeping the central issue before my mind, but goes nowhere near deciding it, if I am told that I must not kill people. It helps because it keeps the question in context and keeps it from becoming a purely technical one in which we seek an answer to the question 'What is a person?' without concern for this particular problem. Displaying a set of alcohol-filled bottles to a biology class I should certainly identify this foetus as the human and that one as the horse, but that problem is different from the one about morality and how to behave.

The second objection is that if the argument works for morals then it must work for law as well. It might seem to be a consequence of my argument, then, that law is not a set of rules but a set of ideals to which the rules only approximate. This does not follow. What the argument about roller-skates shows is that law is made and interpreted in the light of things other than rules, and that legal reasoning is not solely a matter of taking a rule as a major premiss, a description of an action as a minor premiss, and deducing a conclusion. This is not a surprising point. On a deductive model of legal reasoning it is impossible to explain satisfactorily the role in judges' statements of such concepts as 'public policy' or 'discretion'[3], which are fairly common in key judgments, or how judges can argue out such questions as whether a flying boat is a ship or an aeroplane for purposes of insurance. If we examine the whole practice of law we find that rules constitute an important part of that practice, but not the whole of it; judgments call on policies, moral values, and so on in deciding how to apply the law in difficult cases or what the 'intention' of the law-makers was. The argument is easier in the analogous moral case: the values, ideals, and so on called upon apart from the rules are themselves indisputably part of morality, and the invoking of them is indisputably a moral argument.

It might still be objected that whether a foetus is a person is not a moral question but rather a call for a definition and hence some sort of verbal question that merely has to be cleared up before we can feed the information into the ratiocinative machine and get the moral argument started. 'Verbal question', or more commonly 'merely verbal question', is a term frequently used by philosophers in a pejorative way, and my reply to this objection is that *either* whether or not a foetus is a person is not a verbal question *or* some verbal questions are important moral questions. It is at such a point as this that we do need the reminder given by invoking the rule that it is wrong to kill people.

Certainly, to ask whether a foetus is a person in this context is not like asking if a man has walked around a squirrel if he has been north, south, east, and west of a squirrel which has turned so as to face him all the way.[4] Were the question like this, it could be settled by a simple job of clarification: we might merely say that in one sense the man has been around the squirrel and in another sense not. The abortion problem, though, could not be solved by a general agreement that in one sense abortion is justified whenever the mother wants it and in another sense not, because it is a matter of doing one thing or another where the one thing is incompatible with the other. Given the context in which the question is raised, something hangs on whether a foetus is to count as a person in a way in

which nothing hangs on whether or not the man's perambula-
tions are to count as having been around a squirrel. If the
foetus question is answered in one way, then the proposed
action is prohibited by a rule generally agreed to be very
important; if it is answered the other way, then the rule is
irrelevant. Whether or not abortion is properly described as
murder might depend on whether we define 'person' so as to
allow a foetus to be a person, but whether or not we so define it
the abortion will have significant effects on people. Abortion
is important in a way in which walking around squirrels
simply is not, and that makes more hang on the question of
whether or not a foetus is a person than on whether or not the
man walked around the squirrel. On the judgment whether
something is a person depend the judgments that he is a fit
object for praise or blame, that he has claims to just treatment
from others, that he has various *prima facie* rights, and so on.

The point can be made also if we imagine what can be done
in a case in which it matters whether or not the man walked
around the squirrel. Somebody's will might specify that Fred
inherits a fortune if and only if he walked around a squirrel on
or before 6 May 1976; if he did not, the money all goes to a
hospital. If this clause is noticed only after the death of the
testator and is contested in court, then the judges are
unfortunately faced with a verbal unclarity. They might be
able to sort it out by discovering that the point of the clause
was that Fred was once crippled and that his father believed
that he could walk properly if he really tried; what matters
then is Fred's motion rather than the squirrel's. Or they might
simply decide that the matter cannot be determined and, say,
divide the money half and half (a pointlessly literal judgment
of Solomon if carried over to the abortion case). The abortion
problem cannot be resolved that way or it would have been.
The importance of the abortion problem is integral to it, not
something external that has been tacked on as has the will to
Fred's circumambulation. The problem about abortion
cannot be resolved simply by a more careful choice of words;
the obscurity we find in the concept of person here is not
attributable to a slap dash use of the concept, but to the moral
dilemma inherent in the situation in which the concept now
has to be employed.

The judges called upon to say whether Dudley and Stephen had committed murder were faced with a problem which is very similar in important ways, and for them to make an arbitrary decision would have been for them to ignore the problem rather than to solve it. They must make a reasoned decision and, as in all other cases, not just anything counts as a reason. It is simply irrelevant that the judges won at poker last night and feel that it would be nice to spread their joy by releasing the prisoner; it is equally irrelevant that they won by cheating without being found out and now feel guiltily that it would be improper for them to condemn others. Their reasons must be to do with the facts of this case and with what murder is, with why we have the concept and why we classify as murders those killings we do so classify. Such reflections will help to determine how this difficult and previously unclassified case should be classified, and other reflections will not. The case is a problem because it is not a '*merely* verbal question' but one requiring a *reasoned* decision.

In the context of the abortion argument, whether or not a foetus is a person is not a question simply to be left to a decision either way, as are the questions whether the man went around the squirrel and whether a certain intermediate colour is yellow or orange. It is a question on the answer to which too many important matters depend. We might, of course, simply give a definition of 'person' under which it was clear whether a foetus was or was not a person, but even if the definition were agreed to, the argument would continue. As we have seen, we are faced here with a moral problem and not with a mere verbal question about the meaning of 'person'. Because of that, agreement on a definition would simply make us ask whether the rule, set out in terms of the taking of *people's* lives, had the right extension. Is it never permissible to take a person's life, even in self-defence or to save the lives of others from unwarranted attack? Even if the life I take to save others' is my own? Why or why not? Is there no moral objection to the taking of dolphins' lives if dolphins are as intelligent, co-operative, and helpful as they are said to be? If not, why is it not similarly permissible to take the lives of some classes of people? And if there is an objection to the taking of dolphins' lives, is that because of the same rule as prohibits the taking of people's lives, or a different one? May we kill at random outside the human sphere? Why? And what does that reflect about the killing of humans? Agreeing on a perfectly precise definition of the word 'person' does not solve the problem about abortion; it simply recasts the way in which it must be discussed.

This objection that the problem might be solved by supplying a definition of 'person' is closely related to another: if our rules are difficult to apply in the form in which they stand, why cannot we re-write them in terms of the reasons we had for making them? The rule against taking vehicles into the park, for example, would then become a rule against injuring children, making noise that annoyed patients in the hospital, damaging lawns or gardens, and so on. If the rules are re-written in this way then we shall not find ourselves caught up in misleading problems of interpretation about whether roller-skates constitute a vehicle. We shall be faced, instead, with a number of more tractable questions about whether the roller-skates damaged the lawn or made noise to the annoyance of the hospital patients, and these are questions which can be settled by fairly straightforward observation.

The rule about killing could be spelled out in the same sort of way, setting out the reasons for prohibiting killing and thereby setting out the features of a thing that bring it under the protection of the rule. The argument about abortion would thus be reduced to a set of questions about whether the foetus has certain properties, and those questions should be capable of being settled empirically. Questions about whether the foetus was human or alive, if an impasse were reached at these points, would have to be broken down further. Following this procedure, we should get a set of questions which can be settled by straightforward empirical means, or else we should make it plain that linguistic similarities were really hiding the fact that the disputants differed in their moral principles, so that the problem is not really one about the interpretation of a rule but one about which rule to observe.

There are two points to be made in response to this objection. The first is that exactly the same problem will arise with the reformulated rule as arose with the original one; it simply arises in a different place, about different terms. The original point was one about rules, not one specifically about the notion of a person, and problems about the scope of terms in rules arise just as much with the reformulation as with the original. What is to count as injury? Is a child injured if he suffers a severe fright but no physical damage? How severe? What is to count as damage to a lawn? A rule prohibiting noise that annoys patients in the hospital (thereby, presumably, delaying their recovery) is surely not meant to rule out a shouted warning to injury-prone children that a two-ton truck with failed brakes is about to break down the fence and run them over, nor to rule out various lesser cases of a similar kind. Plainly, the list one could make of such problematic cases is an open-ended one. Problems of interpretation could arise with each of these rules and would have to be settled. Making an addition so that the rule prohibited, say, unjustifiable noise is not a move likely to preclude the possibility of argument about interpretation.

Second, if we do manage to reduce the problem to one of which rule I ought to follow, this, like the question 'How far does the rule extend?', raises all the original problems again and therefore fails to solve them. If I want to know which of two rules to adopt it is no good my trying to solve the problem by applying either of them, just as there is no point to my trying to solve the problem of how far a rule ought to extend by applying it. Applying rules will not solve problems about those rules themselves. If I am faced with a clash of moral requirements, putting forward either rule will do no more than remind me of my problem; it will not solve the problem. Any attempt to solve the problem of which rule I ought to follow by reference to Utilitarianism or some similar doctrine would be unsatisfactory in that it would only raise the same sort of problem again. I ought to act for the greatest good of the greatest number, perhaps, but the greatest number of what? All and only people? All and only people who govern their conduct by moral considerations? If dolphins are so intelligent, ought they to be included, too? A rule such as that of Utilitarianism does not solve the problem, because the problem arises again about *its* scope.

If the abortion problem is reduced to a set of questions that can be settled by observation, then the sort of difficulty that I have been discussing does not arise, though the question 'How far does the rule extend?' or 'To which empirical questions can the problem be reduced?' itself involves that sort of difficulty. Where disagreement about the problem can be seen to exist because the protagonists hold different moral principles, though, as they might be said to do if they disagree about the extension of the rule, it might be objected that the difficulty does not arise unless one assumes some sort of absolutist or naturalistic ethical theory. If we take the line, say, that ultimately we simply choose our own moral principles, then it might be concluded that where moral disagreement takes the form of disagreement about general moral rules the matter cannot be settled by invoking rules because it cannot be settled at all. I doubt if this is true. Even if I choose my own moral code as I choose for myself a brand of shaving cream, this sort of problem would be raised occasionally within it and would not obviously be resolvable simply by seeing what followed from the most general rules in my code. If my most general rule, or one of my most general rules, were 'Always be kind,' I must still sort out whether being kind involves being nice to people, dogs, snails, oysters, and carrots, or where, along such a path, the line is to be drawn and why it is to be drawn there. I must also be prepared to raise with myself in certain situations the question of whether it would be kind to be cruel, or in some other way to find myself in a moral quandary about what would count as following the rule. Even within a non-absolutist, non-naturalistic moral code I could have to choose between rules or ponder about the application of a rule, and these activities would still raise the problems that I have described. The alternative is to regard morality as no more than a matter of arbitrary whim.

It might be said, in either an absolutist or a non-absolutist Moral Rule theory, that problems of the sort I have described arise at the level of particular moral rules, but that the problems that arise there are solved by reference to more general moral rules requiring us to be kind, generous, just, and so on. Certainly, it might be conceded that a rule such as that against the taking of human life will sometimes give rise to problems of interpretation, but those problems are to be solved by reference to superior rules in the moral hierarchy, not by looking for something other than rules. But the implication of this objection, that problems about the scope and interpretation of rules do not arise at the most general level, is not true. Indeed, one might well expect that problems of interpretation and application would become greater as the rules became more general. One point of the abortion case is that it raises the question 'What counts as a person?', and that question can be raised no matter how general the rule requiring a certain sort of behaviour towards people. A rule generally requiring me to be just still leaves questions about who or what has claims to just treatment. A question such as 'Does this man have a claim to just treatment from me (given that he has, in the past, shown no signs of considering justice in his relations with me or anybody else)?' is, I take it, obviously a moral question, so the sort of problem that arises out of the abortion case will also arise at levels of greater generality. One cannot solve the problem by referring to rules of greater particularity. That either treats abortion as a mere decision-case like those about squirrels and colours, which I argued earlier to be improper, or removes it from that realm by giving a justification for the more particular rule, a justification which will immediately raise all the problems I have been citing.

The final objection that I want to consider is this: when one has finally worked out the proper scope or interpretation or application of the rule, what one has worked out is what was actually in the rule anyway. One is simply working out the rule, and the decision is still made and justified by applying the rule. Even if the substance of this objection is correct, it will not affect my argument. Working out what is already, perhaps, in the rule (Who has claims to just treatment? Is a foetus the sort of thing that ought not to be killed?) is itself, as we have seen, taking on a moral problem, and it is a moral problem which cannot be solved by applying the rule because it is about the rule. Hence, it is a moral problem the solution to which is not ultimately deduced from a moral rule.

Not very many of our choices about what we ought morally to do are hard cases. Most of them fairly clearly fall under well established moral rules: we must not kill our wives to save the cost of a divorce, and we ought not to snatch an old lady's handbag to get a bus fare and avoid a two-block walk home. The hard cases, though, are genuine moral problems, and the most worrying and the hardest to solve. Any satisfactory moral theory must be able to give some account of them. Theories claiming that morality consists ultimately of rules and that all moral justifications depend on rules can give no such account; in this respect I claim that they have failed.

To make what I take to be the same point in another way, before we can justify something by showing that it comes under a moral rule, we must have some way of telling which rules are moral rules. Moral argument about the rules themselves must be possible. In hard cases and arguments about which rules are moral rules we proceed by invoking virtues and ideals and arguing about their analysis.

Rules are essential to some parts of morality in a quite special way: in some cases it does matter whether or not everybody does the same. There is no value to my keeping promises (if that could be done in the circumstances) or driving on the left unless enough other people keep promises and drive on the left; my act has value only because it is a following of an often-followed rule. That rule is, in such cases, a constituent of the moral situation. Moral philosophers by and large, though, have not been thinking of this sort of rule when they have talked of moral rules. They have been thinking rather of rules which are not part of the moral situation, but which stand over and above the situation simply for use in making judgments about it.

Setting aside rules partly constitutive of the moral situation, it seems clear that, even if at the cost of efficiency, we could employ in the easy cases the sorts of arguments we employ in the hard ones were it necessary to justify our actions in such cases. Moral rules, though no doubt necessary for the everyday practice of morality by at least most people if we are to be at all efficient, would then not be of great importance for moral philosophy and could not play the role so often assigned to them in recent moral philosophy.

NOTES
1   R. v Dudley and Stephens (1884), 14 Q.B.D., 273. See also 'The Case of the Speluncean Explorers', by Lon. L. Fuller, *Harvard Law Review*, 1949.
2   I have in mind, in particular, the work of R.M. Hare and his followers.
3   See, e.g. R. M. Dworkin, 'Is Law a System of Rules?', in *Essays in Legal Philosophy*, ed. R. S. Summers (Basil Blackwell, Oxford, 1968).
4   This example comes from William James, *Pragmatism* (Longmans, Green and Co., London, 1946), p.43.

TWO
One sort of moral rule

It is sometimes said that pain is an evil and ought, therefore, to be avoided whenever possible. It is not really clear that this sets out a reason to avoid causing pain. It appears, rather, to be circular: pain is an evil *in that* one ought not to cause it unnecessarily. There could be some disease which killed people painlessly, but the cure for which was, to as great or small an extent as one might want for the story, painful. It is far from clear, given only these facts in the story, that it would be a better world if sufferers from the disease were simply left to die, or that it is anything but a better world for the discovery of the cure. It certainly seems odd to regard the discovery of the cure as the introduction to the world of an evil, even though of an evil accompanied by a countervailing good; the discovery of the cure is wholly good, though, of course, it does not follow from that that there could be nothing better.

One might even want to argue that pain is sometimes a good thing, and there would certainly be no need to look for esoteric arguments. As one reason, pain can act as a signal to give warning of danger. The child who suffers pain in his hand on reaching out for the flame in a wood fire learns not to put his hand in the fire, and that is a good thing; pain hurts, but the main worry with somebody's putting his hand into a fire is that it will be burned, and, because of the pain, that is avoided. A child who suffers pain in his bottom after pulling his brother's hair might well learn not to indulge himself in that sort of behaviour in the future, and, at least until the child is old enough to be taught that lesson in some other way, that can be a good thing. Suffering pain that can later be expressed in special ways might result in the production of great works of art, and, for some artists, might even be a causally necessary condition of their producing anything worthwhile. The suffering of pain can change one's whole outlook on life; it might produce a previously lacking sympathy with others, or a readiness to reflect on the consequences of what one does rather than simply to act in an irresponsible and flibberty-gibbet manner. In these cases, and many more, pain is, at least apparently, a good thing.

There might be an objection to the claim that these cases show pain to be a good thing. One might want to say that pain is still a drawback, that we put up with it only for its consequences, and that it would be a still better world if we could have those consequences without the pain. That might well be true. It would be a still better world if we could rid a body of cancer by saying three times 'I cure thee', but in the world we live in some other cure for cancer is still a good thing.

That pain can be good instrumentally may not seem to need much demonstration, but the idea that pain is, nevertheless, an evil in itself is a deeply entrenched one that seems to underlie many discussions in moral philosophy. I certainly do not want to claim that pain is good in itself. What I want to argue is that pain is not bad in itself. Certainly pain is unpleasant, but whether the causing of pain exhibits a vice or is immoral depends on other things. What it depends on, as I shall try to show, is not simply a balancing effect, or the question of whether the pain caused was the lesser of two evils, the smaller of two amounts of pain one or other of which must be caused. It depends on other things, such as the point of doing whatever causes the pain, or whether the agent has the right to do whatever causes the pain (as track organisers have the right to arrange a marathon race, the running of which will cause pain to the competitors, or a boxer has the right to try to win his contest).

I do not want to claim that pain is bad only instrumentally. The term 'instrumental' seems far too crude to use in such circumstances. The morality of pain-causing is complicated, but when it is immoral, the reasons why it is immoral lie outside the simple fact that it is a case of causing pain. What is shown by the cases I discuss of pain being instrumentally good is that the notion of pain itself is morally neutral. If a man discovers a cure for cancer and the cure happens to be painful, then we might well continue to look for a less painful cure, but he has not done something evil which we tolerate for the sake of its consequences. The notion of toleration is simply not at home in such circumstances. What he has done is something good.

It should be made clear that my argument here is not directed against Utilitarianism. What I am trying to show is something about the relationship between the concept of pain and moral concepts such as cruelty. That is the limit of my endeavour at this stage. It may be that a Utilitarian or somebody else would use the word 'pain' as I use the word 'cruelty', but that should not affect my argument about the relationship between pain-causing and what ought to be done. In fact, I think that such a person would be using the word 'pain' in a technical sense, or perhaps simply confusedly. Certainly he would make nonsense of many of the things we ordinarily say with the English word 'pain', such as the descriptions I give here of various cases. The marathon runner who causes pain to himself or others by running hard without cheating does nothing wrong. It is perhaps worth stressing again that the doctor who employs the only treatment to cure a serious disease, a painful treatment, does *nothing* wrong. If God had made a better world then the treatment might not be painful, or there might be no such disease, but the doctor works in this world, and there he does nothing wrong. But my argument is about the morality of pain, not about English usage. What I am investigating here is the relationship between the phenomenon of pain, knowingly caused, and such vices as cruelty, and the role that rules might have in that morality. Rules of thumb, I shall argue, can be formed and serve a purpose, but directives such as "Never cause pain" or "Never be cruel", possessing the universality which would enable them, at least in principle, to settle all cases or to serve as major premises in practical syllogisms, are either improper in a way related to falsity or vacuous in a way related to analyticity.

My point here does not rest on the generality of such a rule as 'Never cause pain'. More specific, though still formally universal, rules about the causing of pain might be adopted, but they would not avoid my objections. The main reason for this we have already seen in the earlier discussion of dirtiness: sticking a knife into somebody, or sticking a knife into somebody deliberately, might sometimes be cruel or wrong and sometimes not. The same goes for smiling at them. Deliberately hurting somebody is usually cruel, but not if one does it as a necessary means of self-defence or something of the sort. Deliberately causing pain simply for fun will not, at least straightforwardly, be cruel if I am careful to choose a masochist as the object of my activities. Attempts to account for the concept of cruelty simply by listing its empirical elements are bound to fail, because the list is open-ended and varying. Attempts to deal with the morality of pain-causing by giving rules setting out the circumstances in which pain-causing is improper are bound to fail until the circumstances are set out in terms of a concept such as cruelty, and if the rule becomes 'Don't be cruel' then it is, I shall argue, vacuous. For convenience, I shall continue my argument in terms of general rules, ignoring more specific forms.

The point I have been making about pain might be made clearer by shifting to a case that will be discussed in some detail later. 'Never kill people' has the universality required to settle, in principle, all cases or to serve as a major premiss in a practical syllogism. Its failure is one related to falsity: not all killings of people are improper or to be prohibited. Apart from accidental killings, which are obviously beside this point, killings necessary in self-defence and various other classes are quite proper. 'Never kill people', then, gives the necessary universal guidance, but at the expense of sometimes guiding one in the wrong direction. 'Never commit murder', on the other hand, has the required universality and never guides one in the wrong direction, but the reason that it never guides one in the wrong direction is that is never guides one in any direction at all.

The concept of murder is formed with a practical point, not as a merely theoretical classification of killings. The concept of murder, as we shall see, is formed as the concept of killings to be discouraged, avoided, or prohibited. That is the point of the concept, and is, in that way, built into it. To say 'do not commit murder' is, therefore, merely to add redundant discouragement. In the particular case, it is to say no more than would be said by 'That would be murder'. A rule such as 'Never commit murder' is, therefore, vacuous, and guides us nowhere. What we need to know when the particular problem comes up is whether the proposed killing would be a murder; once we know that it would, we know whether or not we ought to go ahead.

A robber chief might say to his cohorts 'Don't commit murder', meaning that they are to avoid anything that would spur on the search for them or increase the penalties, but he is giving a different sort of advice to people who, in the relevant way, clearly are not concerned about what they ought to do. He is not giving them moral advice. Because they do not feel moral restraint in the recognition that an act would be murder, the moral advice that they should never murder would not guide them either.

For many of the reasons for which pain can be a good thing, it might be a good thing deliberately to inflict pain on somebody. Doing so need not be cruel. If I have to raise my son in circumstances which make him vulnerable to a great and painful danger, my deliberately introducing him to a small amount of the danger and its attendant pain might be the best way of having him avoid the serious danger. If he is too young to understand explanations, it might be the only way. Hitting him when he pulls his brother's hair might save him from being hit harder and a lot more often by older children he could annoy with that habit, and, as a quite separate point, it might eventually result in his being a better person. A doctor or surgeon might have to inflict pain on somebody in order to cure him of some disease or disability. In cases such as these, it is at least not obvious that the deliberate infliction of pain is cruel, and in at least some of the cases it is obvious that it is not cruel. Nor need the reason for its not being cruel be the balancing effect that the deliberately inflicted pain saves the sufferer or others from a greater pain that they would suffer otherwise; the disease from which the surgeon cures his patient might be a painless one, and the danger against which I protect my son might be one inversely proportional to the pain it causes.

Of course, arthritis can remove the delight from a game of tennis and suffering might produce a misanthrope rather than a person of great understanding and sympathy. I do not claim that pain is necessarily good, nor even that it is always good. In those cases described above in which pain does seem to be a good thing, I do not claim that pain necessarily produces those consequences that make it a good thing. I have simply described the way the world is in some cases. That seems an appropriate thing to do, because the claim that pain is evil is, at least *prima facie*, a substantive and synthetic claim which ought to be tested against the facts of life. If somebody does want to say that it is analytically true that pain is an evil, the cases that I have described will at least be a lot more difficult to explain and understand in ordinary terms. Pain is neither an evil nor a good; it is simply a part of the world in which we live, sometimes good and sometimes not.

The danger from which I protect my son might not be quite so great as I have suggested, and the pain that it causes might be quite considerable. The danger of his falling down a flight of well-made stairs is probably not sufficient to justify informing him of it with the pain involved in throwing him down the last few steps, even if that is the only way. In more complicated and more likely cases, though, it might not be at all clear whether or not the warning and consequent care is worth the pain that it involves. In such a case it does seem important, if I go ahead, that it is my son with whom I am dealing; I stand in a special relationship to him. My inflicting that pain on other people's children, though, even for the same good end, is a different thing altogether. If I do that, I am inflicting pain on somebody in pursuit of purposes it is not my business to attain, and that fact makes a difference. In the same way, even if suffering produces great art, it is not my business to cut a man's ear off so that he will produce something with which I can decorate my lounge room. The same applies in a range of cases which do not involve the infliction of pain. The objection is not to the pain as such, which is simply part of the world, but to my interfering in somebody else's affairs. My inflicting similar pain on somebody else, or somebody else's inflicting the same pain on that person, might be something to which no moral objection could properly be raised. The morality of cases involving pain is a good deal more complex than is suggested by the remark that pain is an evil.

What is objectionable about the infliction of pain is not always that it is unnecessary. If I take up the running of marathon races I shall make myself suffer a great deal of pain, but that is nobody's business but my own even if I take up the running only as a way of filling in an idle half-hour before dinner, in which case the pain I suffer is really quite unnecessary. The fact that this is a case of self-inflicted pain might be misleading, because the point does not depend on that. If I should become good enough at running to make others run harder and suffer more in order to beat me, then I cause them more and unnecessary pain, but what I do is surely not evil or subject to any moral censure. On the other hand, even if it is very well established that I can beat somebody else in the marathon every time, even though he keeps on trying to make up the difference and drives himself as hard as he can in the race, and causes himself enormous suffering, if I should stamp on his foot at the start, causing him just enough pain to make him drop out of the race and saving him all the pain that he would suffer if he ran, then what I do surely is subject to moral censure. The difference between these cases lies not in the necessity or the amount of pain, but in whether I had a right to do whatever it was that caused the pain.

A surgeon might, if caught on a ship at sea or stuck in the Arctic when the huskies have run away with the sled carrying the relevant equipment, sometimes have to operate without anaesthetic. If the case is an emergency, then a surgeon who simply cannot bear the thought of causing pain would be a good deal less use than one who positively enjoyed it, but all that shows is that there are two ways of failing to have a virtue. Causing more pain than was reasonably necessary might result in the second doctor's being cast out from his profession, so he might be very careful not to overstep the bounds of propriety and cause unnecessary pain. Nevertheless, it is plain that he needs to be watched and that we need to have rules under which he could be struck off if he acted improperly; he causes no unnecessary pain, but his attitude to pain is reprehensible and means that unfavourable moral judgments could properly be passed upon him. He enjoys causing pain; it is one of his aims.

The morality of cases involving pain is various and complicated. Sometimes it is a good thing, sometimes bad, and, when it is bad, the vice that is exhibited need not be cruelty. The surgeon who prefers cases when anaesthetic is unavailable is cruel, the man who simply does not care one way or the other whether people suffer as he sets about achieving his aims is callous and inhuman, the man to whom it never occurs that others may suffer as a result of his activities is thoughtless and inconsiderate, the man who never notices that people are suffering is insensitive, the marathon runner who stamps on his rival's foot is unfair and a cheat, and the man who cuts off the ear of a potential artist is arrogant, interfering, and lacking in concern for the rights and freedom of others. Cases involving the deliberate infliction of pain are often evil, but they can be so in a number of different ways which are confused if we simply say that pain is an evil. Sometimes the deliberate infliction of pain is a good thing. Pain itself is morally neutral; its morality lies outside it, in such concepts as kindness, cruelty, and humanity.

People can be cruel to be kind, but it would be wrong to take this as blurring the claim that cruelty is a vice. That particular phrase is a special one that should be hyphenated as cruel-to-be-kind. That somebody is cruel-to-be-kind does not entail that he is cruel; in such a case it would be grossly misleading, and possibly actionable to say simply that he was cruel. The opposite of the 'cruelty' he displayed is not kindness, but squeamishness.

The concepts that we have are instruments for discrimination in the world we live in, and they arise as a response to the rubbing together of our needs or interests and that world. We have lots of different sorts of concepts because there are lots of different sorts of interests and lots of different sorts of reasons for which we need to discriminate. We distinguish between people and inanimate objects, for example, because it would be quite improper to treat the two in the same ways; it would be very nasty to make a person wearing only a fig-leaf stand on one foot in the middle of a snow-covered park right throughout the winter. The discrimination is not an arbitrary one, of course, and we cannot place things in either category willy-nilly or make a statue a person by dressing it or taking it breakfast in bed. We distinguish between them because they are different; people can feel cold, be embarrassed, or get tired, and statues cannot. But it is these differences that come to mind and not others such as that statues are harder to the touch and have no need to file their finger nails, because a point of the distinction is a moral one to which the former facts are relevant and the latter not. For some purposes, such as the distribution of weight in an aeroplane, there are no relevant differences between people and statues, and in such circumstances we can conceptualise them both simply as physical objects.

We need to distinguish people from things other than statues, and we need to raise questions about them other than whether to leave them shivering in the park through the winter. Because our concepts arise in terms of our needs in this world, very unusual cases can be difficult to place under a concept. Cases of the merely logically possible can fail to raise genuine questions and sometimes serve to indicate ways in which our concepts can operate only because the world is as it actually is. There is no real reason to believe that the criterion for personal identity is either something such as a mental history tied together by memory or something such as spatio–temporal continuity of the body; in the world in which our concept of person was formed and in which it operates, these two criteria, as a matter of fact, go together, or at least do not run counter to each other. That it is logically possible that a case should arise in which they did run counter to each other does not affect the operability of the concept of person in this world.

If we discovered one day that all the memories formerly associated with Fred Bloggs are now associated with the body formerly regarded as Bill Smith's, there is no reason to believe that the resultant entity is Smith, Bloggs, Smoggs, or Blith; our concept of person was not formed and is not equipped to deal with that sort of case, so we can tell the long story of what happened but make no short remark about which person has continued through the incident. Such a case need show nothing about the primacy of either mental or physical criteria in the concept of person. Our concepts grow up out of our interaction with the world and our worries about it; that mental and physical criteria can be logically distinguished, if they can, does not mean that they are distinguished in a concept dealing with the world in which we live in fact. This is one of the ways in which our concept can, quite properly, be imprecise.

If our concept of person is imprecise in these areas, then it might be made more precise. New experiences to be categorised might determine the concept in a variety of ways where it is now quite open-ended. If we somehow became aware of disembodied existence after death, then the concept of a person might become determined by non-physical criteria. The concept of a soul might be an attempt at such a determination. But this would not be *the* determination of the concept of person, because biologists, physiologists, town planners and others each have an interest in persons which might lead to a different determination of the concept. We should then have several different relatively precise concepts where we now have the one imprecise concept of person, but none of those new concepts would be the concept of person. Because they have diverged in different and incompatible ways from the concept we now have, no one of them could be regarded simply as *the* concept of person further developed, though each of them could be regarded as a new concept developed from the concept of person. Those new concepts, therefore, would not help with our question about personal identity, though they might result in that question's being replaced by a number of different ones. The problem about personal identity might be that, because the concept of person was formed in terms of certain common actual experiences and interests, it is undetermined with respect to other experiences and interests, and that different determinations with respect to the different interests might give us different questions with different answers. But the concept of person we now have might still serve a useful function for, say, a town planner or somebody concerned with how he ought to treat his neighbours. For somebody with those interests, the respects in which the concept of person is undetermined might not matter.

Other cases may be empirically possible but crop up only comparatively rarely, in which case the prime concept may be imprecise with repect to such cases, but they may be dealt with by the formation of a special concept. The concept of a monstrous birth or a sport serves such a function. Similarly, the discovery of new facts about something may make it unclear whether a concept applies to it because of some imprecision in the concept. If the concept of a person is the sort of mixture that I suggested above, then we might well expect some doubt about the status of dolphins after the fairly recent discoveries about their intelligence, and in fact the eating of dolphins has been made illegal in some places because it smacks of cannibalism. If computers are made which can do all those little things failure to do which lead to matter of fact objections to the claim that people are computers, then there might well be a temptation to say, not merely that people are computers, but that some computers are people.

Our concept of person grew up in a world which lacked those computers and did not know those facts about dolphins. It deals easily with the larger contrasts between people and eels or motor cars, but as we see similarities between people and dolphins or computers, similarities relevant to the question of whether they ought to be accorded the respect and rights accorded to people, it becomes less clear how the concept of person applies. The concept grows up in response to the problems that we face, and centres around standard cases. Difficulties about the application of the concept arise with less standard cases, or when something which was not previously a problem for one reason or another becomes one. In such cases, special concepts are often formed to mark the cases off. So we have the concepts of moron and living vegetable applying to people and clearly marking them off as sub-standard instances, and we have the concept of a foetus which might or might not apply to something that is also a person (or a horse or whatever). A normal adult is the standard case of a person, but a foetus is not; the question about a foetus arises when abortion becomes a problem.

There are many different reasons, and different sorts of reasons, for distinguishing one sort of thing from another, and these reasons shape the concepts that grow up to perform these discriminatory tasks. These reasons for the discrimination give a point to the concept, and that point is central to any analysis we may give of the concept. It determines what counts as an instance of the concept and what does not. One point of the concept of person, *the* point in the context of abortion, is that people deserve to be treated in certain ways, or perhaps not to be treated in certain ways. To shift from asking whether the foetus may be aborted to asking whether the foetus is a person is simply to ask the same question in a different way, and it does not break it down into smaller ones or advance the argument in any way; one point about the concept of person is that people deserve certain sorts of treatment, in particular that they deserve immunity against having their lives wantonly terminated, and that is the point that makes this particular re-phrasing of the question appropriate. Other points about people are irrelevant in this context except insofar as they bear on this one, so the re-phrasing of the question cannot make any logical step in the argument. If it is not clear how the reasons for discriminating lead us to classify an X, then it is not clear whether the concept in question applies to X.

The reasons for discriminating in a given way determine whether a concept applies in a given case, and items with no empirical properties in common may come under the same concept. A cheque, a motor yacht, or a promise to reform may all be birthday presents, and the empirical properties of even the giving might differ in the three cases: the cheque might be handed over in person, the papers for the yacht (not the yacht itself) sent by mail, and the promise simply made by word of mouth. Despite their lack of any common empirical properties, all three cases have the same significance or meaning, that is, we have reasons for classifying them together. Those reasons are the point of the concept of gift. There might be reasons for distinguishing between them, too; the cheque and the promise might have different effects on the recipient's tax status, but then we are considering them as income and not as gifts. The same situation can be broken up and classified in different ways in accordance with different interests.

Not all concepts arise from wants or needs or interests that everybody has. Some concepts are quite specialised and some have very technical points. The income tax assessor, with his own particular professional interests, might give a quite technical point to the concept of gift and operate that notion in a slightly different way from the rest of us. He might, for example, treat something given towards the upkeep of an aged relative as being not a gift even if it is given on the relative's birthday, but treat as a gift the same thing given to a person similar in all respects except for not being a relative. The point of his discrimination is clearly different from, though related to, ours. The concept of a first day cover arises in response to the particular interests of philatelists, and the concept of castling or queen's rook arises in response to the interests of chess players. These interests, though inter-personal and translatable from one person to another, are quite special. Such interests give rise to special concepts, and if the interests and problems are very precise, as they might be in mathematics, then the concepts arising in response to them will be similarly precise, unlike the concept of person.

Our tax assessor, with his special interests, created a concept very closely related to one of ours. Interests can overlap; it makes a difference to either a philatelist or a person posting a letter whether or not a stamp has been cancelled, though it doesn't make the same difference to each. The same concept or set of items can answer to more than one of our wants, needs, or interests, and then we have a concept with more than one point. Biologists and people in general have an interest in human beings, and biologists and people in general have an interest in the foetus. A biological interest in people or foetuses is not the same as a moral interest (which does not mean that a biologist ought not to consider the moral implications of his work; that somebody is a biologist does not mean that he has, or ought to have, only biological interests), so the concepts have different points. A biologist's being able to say quite clearly whether a foetus is human (rather than, say, equine), is therefore quite compatible with its being unclear whether a foetus is human (rather than whatever) when the question is considered with the different interests of somebody concerned about abortion. Answering the biologist's question, because it calls on different sorts of reasons, does nothing toward answering the other question.

As a matter of fact, some things are dangerous; they cause loss of life or limb, or financial collapse, or depression, or whatever. In the standard case, these things are to be avoided, and that is why we classify them together. The concept of danger has the point of guiding our actions by warning us against these things. This does not mean that nobody can act against the guidance and seek danger or attempt suicide, but a red-lettered sign by the river saying 'Danger' is neither a pointless piece of information chosen at random nor an invitation to swim. Some people are odd, but the concept of danger is formed inter-personally in terms of the interests of people in general, and those interests lie in the avoidance of danger. That some people, for the thrill of rebellion, fish only near signs saying 'Fishing Prohibited' does not mean that those signs are not intended to guide action in a different direction.

Most of our concepts probably are action-guiding in one way or another, though it does not follow that they guide action in only one direction without further information about the wants or interests of those involved. We can note as an interesting but presently useless piece of information that something is flammable. The point of having that concept, though, or the point of especially picking out those properties coming under it, is that they are important in guiding some of our activities. They are, indeed, sufficiently important for the word to have been deliberately changed from 'inflammable' to 'flammable' so as to reduce the possibility of confusion. Fire plays an important part in some of our activities because it is very useful and very dangerous; we sometimes want it and we somethimes need to avoid it. It is the role of these facts in guiding our actions one way or another that gives point to the concept of flammability. Other concepts have the point of guiding our actions in one direction only: concepts such as warning, prohibition, and requirement.

Amongst those concepts which have the especially action-guiding point of heading us in one direction rather than leaving us to go one way or another depending on how we feel are those loosely categorised as moral concepts. We can be rebellious by ignoring a 'Fishing Prohibited' sign or pay people back by being cruel only because that sign and that concept point us in the other direction; it is refusal to be guided, not merely unorthodox action, that is rebellious. Because a concept such as cruelty is action-guiding in this way, marking something off as not to be done, an objection that I have been cruel cannot be met simply by saying that I wanted to be cruel; that leaves the situation as one in which I have done what ought not to be done and shown myself to be nasty. If it is pointed out to me in a cautionary tone of voice that the material I have picked up is flammable, I can reply that I am about to cook dinner and need something flammable in order to do so; I have been guided in the appropriate way by the concept. But when somebody tells me that what I have done is cruel, I can show that I have been guided in the appropriate way by the concept only if I show that he is mistaken; I must show that my action was not really cruel because I correctly believed that it would not cause the pain somebody else might expect, or because it was the only way to cure somebody of a serious disease or make him see the error of his ways, or something of that sort. Part of the point of the concept of cruelty is that what comes under that concept is wrong and ought not to be done.

The tax assessor changed the concept of gift by giving it a new and rather formal or legalistic point. The same thing can be done to moral concepts. The law might give formal definitions of murder and cruelty, and these legal concepts might differ from those normally employed. In some cases, bad drafting of a law might lead to there being a difference. With the best drafting that could be done, it might be impossible to frame a law against cruelty both so that proof was possible in all or most of the clearly cruel cases and so that all those cases we should want excluded from the ambit of the law were excluded. Law-making requires formal setting out of rules, consideration of how offences might be proven, questions about whether the enforcement of a given rule would cause more trouble than it would save, and so on. Such problems give to the legislator concerns which are not present in the moral case and mean that legal concepts frequently differ from related moral concepts because they respond to those different needs and have different points.

In terms of these legal concepts we *can* ask whether murder or cruelty are wrong, but that does not go against my claim that part of the ordinary notion of cruelty is that what is cruel is wrong. When I sensibly say of somebody 'I know that what he did was cruel, but was it wrong?', the question can be translated into one such as 'I know he is guilty under the Cruelty to Animals Act, but was he really cruel?', and when I ask whether cruelty is wrong, that question can be translated into one about just how far the legal concept of cruelty coincides with the moral concept. We might say of somebody in a moral case that he had been cruel but it was not really wrong if we meant that he ought to be excused, say, because he had suffered excessive provocation, but his being excused is appropriate only if he has done something that he ought not to have done. An attempt to show that his act was justified, on the other hand, would be an attempt to show that it was not really cruel but rather, say, cruel-to-be-kind.

It is a matter of fact that the world is as it is; it might have been different. If suffering always produced great insights, art of high merit, and moral development, and only suffering produced those things, then our ideas about what ought to be done would be different from what they are. It is a matter of fact, and not of necessity, that those qualities of character which constitute cruelty do constitute a vice, even though it is analytically true that cruelty is a vice. We gather together under the concept of cruelty certain attitudes to human suffering because they are anti-social and ought to be avoided. Those same reasons or that same point to the concept, could lead us in a different world to bring quite different attitudes to human suffering under the concept of cruelty. If pain, and pain alone, produced insight, art, and moral development, then a delight in causing pain would be socially desirable and would constitute the virtue of kindness; a delight in giving pleasure and an unwillingness to cause pain would be the vice of cruelty. What comes under the concept of cruelty in the one case is quite different from what comes under it in the other case, as a motor yacht is quite different from a promise to reform, but we can see that it is the concept of cruelty both times because the point of classifying those qualities of character together is the same in both cases. It is synthetic that a delight in causing pain is cruel, but analytic that what is cruel ought not to be done.

It is because what is cruel ought not to be done that a situation in which one is forced to be cruel is so difficult and leaves one feeling torn. Being forced to cause pain where that is not cruel is not at all the same sort of problem. The surgeon faced by an armed man who says "I don't care about your golf, perform this painful operation necessary to save my child's life or I shall shoot you", should feel no compunction about performing the operation and would be a fool if he did not. The surgeon faced by an armed man who says "Give all these people severe electric shocks so that I can hear them scream or I shall shoot you", might well feel compunction. If he refused to succumb to the threats he might be a martyr, but he would not be a fool. If it is not true that cruelty ought always to be avoided, then the particular nastiness of a situation in which somebody is forced to be cruel cannot be explained. The situation is so nasty because one is being forced to do what is wrong (if the threat were to the second surgeon's family rather than to him, he might be regarded as being forced to do something wrong whichever he chose), and that is why such situations lead to a feeling of being torn.

If we take it that cruelty is, analytically, a vice, then the claim that cruelty is wrong will be true, vacuous, and completely ineffective as a moral rule or principle or any sort of guide to action. Being told that cruelty is wrong when we are wondering what to do is like being told that $2 + 2 = 4$ when we want to know how many bottles of beer remain in the refrigerator. Being told that cruelty is wrong makes no substantive move in the game at all; we need to know what is cruel in the given circumstances. The point of moral rules is that they should guide our conduct, but the remark that cruelty is wrong is like a direction-post which says merely 'Make sure that you take the correct turning' without indicating which way lies Booligal and which way lies Hay.

The rule that one must not (unnecessarily) cause pain is quite different and might count as a rough and ready guide to what counts as cruelty in the world in which we find ourselves. It can be a rule in a way in which the remark about cruelty's being wrong cannot, because it is substantive and rules out some straightforwardly identifiable courses of action. It is like being told that one cannot castle across check as compared with being told that on one's tenth move one must either castle or not castle.

Furthermore, the rule that one ought not unnecessarily to cause pain is, by and large, a good guide. Causing pain will often be cruel, acting without any care for whether we are causing unjustifiable pain is callous, and so on. The point of the concept of pain is that it marks off something we want to avoid, and that gives it an especially close relationship to moral concepts which amounts to a rebuttable presupposition that pain ought not to be caused. This is one of the reasons why, when causing pain is bad, it is not accurately describable as merely instrumentally bad. Because we want to avoid pain, a willingness or desire to cause it, and indifference to whether it is caused, or a constant failure to consider whether it will be caused are all socially undesirable and make inter-personal relationships harder to operate smoothly.

The causing of pain will often be cruel, callous, inhumane, inconsiderate, or insensitive, and all of these are vices. So here is a good candidate for a moral rule. It is a *moral* rule because the reasons given in support of it are moral reasons, specifically that infringement is likely to display one of several vices; it would be a maxim of prudence or a law of the land if different reasons were given in support of it. But it cannot play the role in which moral rules have so frequently been cast by philosophers because it is not universal. To put the point another way, if the claim that causing pain (unnecessarily) is wrong is taken as a universal claim and not as a rough generalisation, then it is false. We may not want pain, but it is rather like spinach; it is sometimes necessary and sometimes good for us. The surgeon may have to hurt me to cure me; I may be so upset at losing the last remaining scholarship to you that I ache; if I run the marathon faster, then you will have to run faster and suffer more in order to beat me. For all those reasons canvassed earlier, it simply is not true that causing pain, even unnecessarily, is always wrong. The moral rule that one ought not unnecessarily to cause pain is a rule of thumb only, though a very good rule of thumb. It will not function properly as a major premise in a deductive model of moral reasoning.

Nor will it serve to provide us with a probability argument as a guide in the difficult cases. That causing pain is normally wrong does nothing to show that it is even probably wrong in exceptional cases. Causing pain is not an evil in itself; when it is an evil, it is so because of all the surrounding circumstances. That causing pain is wrong in normal circumstances, even that it is always wrong in normal circumstances, gives no guidance to behaviour in exceptional cases, because what makes a case exceptional is that the circumstances are odd and importantly different. What makes a case exceptional is that the circumstances that normally make the guide a good one no longer obtain.

THREE
The other sort of moral rule

If some moral rules, such as the rule that one ought to avoid causing pain, are rules of thumb, it is nevertheless true that other moral rules have a quite different function and should guide our behaviour in a quite different way. There are rules such as that one ought to keep one's promises. What marks these moral rules off from the others is not their being 'universal', or its being the case that it is never morally proper for anybody to break a promise, but the way in which they enter into moral reasoning through their roles in practices or institutions.

That I have made a promise does, other things being equal, give me a reason for doing what I promised to do, but it is not a reason which prevails no matter what. If I have promised to meet Bertha outside the Kadena Koffee Shop at 4.30 and, when rushing there at 4.25, find a young maiden tied to the railway line and a mustachio-twirling, dark-suited villain disappearing over the horizon, then I ought to stop and release her even though doing so means failure to keep my promise to Bertha. I ought to stop and release her for the same reason as I ought otherwise to have kept my promise to Bertha: failure to do so shows the vice of injustice by exhibiting a lack of concern for the rights and legitimate interests of others. If a given action that causes pain, such as running faster in the marathon, is permissible, then the rule that one ought not to cause pain is irrelevant and has no bearing on the situation; if one considers all the details of fact and argument about a pain-causing situation, eschewing short cuts in the reasoning, then the rule that one ought not to cause pain is otiose. If I make a promise, though, then that fact and the rule that I ought to keep my promises are never irrelevant or otiose; they always provide a reason for doing whatever it is that I have promised to do. The reason need not be a final one and can be overridden, but, if it is not to be a final one, it needs to be overridden and therefore to be considered.

The nature and workings of practices are important to my argument and are commonly misunderstood; it is important that at least some of the misunderstandings should be removed. The two things about practices that I particularly need to explain for the rest of my argument are what a practice is and how it generates obligations. Since the term 'practice' is, as used here, something of a technical term, it might seem odd that I should complain that those who have used it before me have misunderstood it. If they introduced the term, how could they be wrong about what it means? But to ask whether stipulative definitions can be wrong is not, in fact, merely a rhetorical question. For one thing, the major writers about practices[1] have not given a formal definition of the term. More important, they have been confused about what sort of things could have the significance which they want to attribute to practices, or about how such things as promising, taken as examples of practices, have the moral significance that they do have. Even if one did stipulate a definition of 'practice', one could not stipulate that what one described had the significance that one wanted it to have.

Practices concern the organisation of, or relationships between, people, constituting an established way of doing something and affecting what justice requires in a given situation. If that is true, then it is plain that practices can be understood only within and in terms of a prior morality; they cannot themselves constitute the base of morality or impose moral requirements independent of the morality within which they operate. This should not be surprising. The term 'practice' was not chosen haphazardly, and 'moral practice' is not all one word. A practice is a habit or custom or established way of doing something, so we say that a man makes a practice of learning a new word each day or talk of the practices of the courts within a given legal system. A moral practice is a practice which generates moral obligations, and to understand what a moral practice is, is to understand how it can generate the obligations. How can a practice take on that moral significance?

Mere common action of any sort does not generate obligations and does not amount to a moral practice. If I make a practice of going along to watch a football match each

Saturday afternoon, or if a very large number of people does so, that practice does not amount to a moral practice and imposes no obligation on anybody either to watch the football match this Saturday or to stay away. It could not be the basis of any reasonable claim that one person made upon another. The situation seems, intuitively, somewhat different if, instead of being one of the spectators, I am one of a team participating in the football match. If members of the team conscientiously turn up to play each Saturday despite the facts that it is sometimes raining and that they sometimes have headaches after a Friday night on the town, then, intuitively, it seems that they would have a basis for a claim against me that I should play despite the fact that I was out on the town last night and do not really feel in the mood. Is the difference merely intuitive, or can we set out a relevant distinction between the two cases? One point of difference between them stands out: as far as being a spectator goes I can take care of myself, but I can be a member of a team only in co-operation with others. In the case described, I have been able to have the fun of playing football only because they have made sacrifices and turned out to play. Now they can have their fun only if I make a sacrifice and play.

The element of co-operation in the second case enables the concept of justice to get a grip, and that, in turn, makes it possible for obligations to emerge from the relationships between the people concerned. The football team or club is, in this respect, a microcosm of larger inter-personal activities that depend on co-operation. Justice is concerned with the proper distribution of benefits and burdens, and it should be fairly clear how it applies in this situation. I want benefits which I can gain only with the co-operation of others, or which, perhaps, I do in fact only gain with the co-operation of others, because that is the most efficient way of doing it, even though I could otherwise have gained the benefits in a less efficient way working by myself. The point of the activity, then, is to produce benefits satisfying needs or wants by co-operating in our work, from which it follows that both needs or wants and works will be relevant to the proper determination of who can make which claims on whom.

If I claim a share of the benefits that come from the

co-operative enterprise, I thereby lay myself open to claims of justice that I shall contribute my share to the work, or that when my turn comes around I shall make the sacrifices necessary for the benefits to be produced. My recognising and meeting the claims on me for work is, *prima facie,* the ground of my claim to a share in the benefits. If I have not contributed to the work and still want to claim a share in the benefits, I should at least have to argue something such as that I was holding myself in readiness to do so but was never called upon (as a soldier in peace time might defend his claim to be paid), or that I should have contributed had it not been for a specific disability beyond my control (as somebody might claim sick pay) and that I do contribute to a larger co-operative enterprise subsuming this one, or something of the sort. That nebulous entity the National Economy might be regarded as a co-operative enterprise subsuming many others. When I work hard all week co-operating with others to produce chicken feed, I do not want merely chicken feed in return. If chicken feed were all I got, I should refuse to do the work. I work hard in the feed factory on the understanding that I can exchange what I produce there for things produced in other enterprises, that is, that the co-operative enterprise I work in is co-operatively related with other co-operative enterprises in the national economy.

In the absence of a special explanation, it is the work that I do in the enterprise on which is based my claim to a share in the benefits produced by the enterprise. If I claim a share in the benefits then I must, in justice, meet the claims made upon me to contribute to the work. In terms of the football team, if I make a claim against others that they shall play even if they do not feel like it when the time comes, and if that is the basis on which the team runs, then I must recognise such a claim when it is made on me.

Whether I ought to hand over some money to you might well depend on something such as whether you had loaned me some; what justice requires of one or allows one to do depends on how others behave. Sometimes it does make a difference whether everybody else does the same. An act which is, if taken by itself, in no way wrong can become wrong if it is at variance with a general practice. My act of buying my son

Charlotte's Web after saying to him 'I promise that I will buy you *Charlotte's Web*' has no particular moral value unless there is a practice or institution of promising, which requires a fairly high incidence of other people's doing what they say they will do after uttering the words 'I promise'.

If there were no such practice, I could decide to do something *like* introducing it for myself: I could make sure that whenever I preceded a remark about my future behaviour with the (puzzling to other people) words 'I promise', I went on to do whatever I had said I would do. Should I fail to do so, I might subject myself to all sorts of hardship. But that does not by itself introduce a practice of promising. It imposes no obligation on me, and it does not make my act either right if I do what I 'promised' to do or wrong if I fail to do so. The utterance of the sounds is not magic, and it requires a certain context before it can take on significance; the word 'promise' has its meaning because *we* have the symbolic act of promising. If, in the way I have suggested, I act alone to introduce the word 'promise', my wife has no reason to be especially impressed if I point out that, in response to my son's desire to go skating, I had said 'I shall take you' and prefaced that by saying 'I promise'. I might as well have prefaced the remark by saying 'Gesundheit' for all the bearing it has on whether I should cut the grass instead. Nor should my son feel let down since I might just as well have prefaced the remark by saying 'Perhaps'. By merely uttering the sounds 'I promise', I do not place myself under any obligation. If I try to introduce promising by myself, making promises only to myself, saying 'I promise' would be like saying 'I will' rather than 'I shall'; it might express a special resolve, but it gives nobody a claim against me.

To place myself under an obligation I must make a promise, and that is an activity requiring inter-personal conventions. Promising is a practice and depends on fairly wide acceptance of the rule that we ought to do what we say we will do after uttering the words 'I promise'. The fairly wide acceptance of the rule affects the morality of what I do after saying 'I promise', and then essaying some remark about my future behaviour, in a way in which the general acceptance of a rule against kicking dogs does not affect the morality of kicking dogs. If kicking dogs is wrong, then it is wrong no matter how many people fail to recognise the fact. But we cannot sensibly say that, if promise-breaking is wrong, it is wrong no matter how many people fail to recognise the fact; if enough people fail to recognise the fact, then promise-making and promise-breaking become impossible. The word 'promise' loses its significance. The rule that we ought to do what we promise to do, unlike the rule that we ought not to kick dogs, does not serve only as a standard against which to judge people's behaviour in a moral situation. It is one of the constituents of the moral situation because it informs one of the ways in which we co-operate.

This account of the morality of promising is intended as an explanation of why we ought to keep promises, and not as a suggestion that we have an obligation to make promises or to have the practice at all. Keeping promises is a good thing to do and breaking promises bad, but having the practice of promising is, _prima facie_, simply useful. Breaking a promise may be unjust, but a group of people shows no injustice in not having the practice of promising at all. What I am concerned with here is the morality inside practices. The reasons for having a practice will usually be non-moral, primarily that it is simply useful. Some co-operative practices (such as government insurance schemes, perhaps) might be introduced for moral reasons such as that they are thought to be required by justice, but such facts about why a practice was instituted are irrelevant to how and why obligations are generated within the practice. Somebody might make a practice of giving money to charity, and a very commendable practice it might be, but the practice is not co-operative, generates no obligations (even amongst the recipients if it is genuine charity), and is not a case of a moral practice as I am using the term here. A moral practice is one that generates obligations, not a practice which is morally good.

By saying 'I promise', I make a promise and place myself under an obligation. It is the creation of the obligation that turns the utterance of the sounds into the making of a promise. If everybody else subjects himself to a rule requiring that he keep his promises even in cases in which it is to his disadvantage to do so, does so to my benefit, and does so on the understanding that I shall do the same (an understanding that I give whenever I buy into the institution by using the words 'I promise' in the relevant circumstances), then it is only just that I should so subject myself as well. This is a case of what has been called commutative obligation, which rests on commutative justice. If I join in a practice and willingly accept the benefits of other people's restricting their behaviour in the ways that the practice requires, then I an under an obligation similarly to restrict my behaviour. To accept the benefit and refuse to contribute my mite is to fail to fulfil an obligation and is unjust.

I cannot, simply by doing some work and then saying that somebody else can claim or could have claimed that work from me, lay the basis for a claim of my own that I can then make on somebody else. If I unsolicitedly scratch your back, you might be ungrateful but are not unjust if you refuse to scratch mine. That is not co-operation. I cannot co-operate by myself, so I cannot generate the claim of a moral practice by myself. My activities cannot generate claims without a context that gives them a special significance, makes them describable in terms of an enterprise involving others, and makes them describable as a contribution to co-operation.

What is needed in order to give them the relevant significance is an established way of doing things in terms of which claims that people make on one another will be understood. Since I cannot co-operate by myself, I cannot establish by myself the way of co-operating. I can, though, suggest forms of co-operation or ways of doing things to which the other people might agree. So there must be an established way of doing things, or, if one wanted to use a formal and sometimes misleading model, one might say that there must be a rule, for there to be a practice which can generate claims and obligations. One person cannot introduce the established way of doing things or the claims and obligations by himself. That must be an inter-personal matter. Consent is one method of establishing the way of doing something, though it is also true that some practices, such as promising, themselves deal with formal or symbolic ways of consenting.

Talk of an established way of doing something suggests a

form of organisation hallowed by time, but it has already been made plain that a long history is not required; consent can establish a way of doing something in a moment, as in 'You wash the dishes and I shall dry'. If Farmer Jones helps Farmer Winterbottom to dig a well, then it might be a matter of custom that such activity is a ground for claims. Farmer Jones, for example, might be able to make a claim on Farmer Winterbottom for help with the harvesting or that he milk the cows when the Jones family goes to the seaside for a holiday. There might be no such custom, though, and the whole thing might be established by agreement on the spot: so much work for a certain return. When the agreement is made, the way of doing things is established; Winterbottom has a claim that Jones shall do so much work, and Jones has a claim that Winterbottom shall do something for him.

Co-operation is always inter-personal, a matter of several people doing something and not simply a matter of individual action by a lone person. His co-operating might consist of his pressing a button every thirty seconds, driving a tractor, or putting his rubbish in a bin rather than strewing it around the yard, and each of these things he could do without other people, but insofar as each of those things is *all* that he is doing, he is not co-operating. Insofar as he is co-operating his activities must be describable in other ways such as, say, helping to make lawn-mowers, helping to plough a field, or helping to keep the yard tidy. In each case the redescription places him in context with the others whom he is helping. One man might sow wheat, another reap it, another grind it, another bake bread; others still might grow spinach, care for and sometimes slaughter the cows, or spend time in a laboratory trying to invent a more effective fertiliser. Each man is doing something different from the others, but each can also be described as doing the same thing: contributing to the production of food. Insofar as they are doing the same thing, they may be co-operating. Context, and the effect it has on the propriety of descriptions of what is going on, can be all-important in determining whether what faces us is a case of co-operation. Considered in a broad context, two boxers might be co-operating, in terms of their contract, to earn a living by beating the daylights out of each other. Considered in the much narrower context of what goes on in the ring, their co-operating with each other would mean that the fight was fixed.

Co-operation is always a matter of having several people doing something, but having more than one person is not sufficient. More than one person goes in for hiking, but it does not follow that they are co-operating with each other. Each simply goes hiking, even when half a dozen people go hiking together. We then have a case of half a dozen people doing the same thing, but no dependence of each on the others. If five drop by the wayside, and the sixth continues alone, he is still hiking; what we had was a collection of six individual cases of hiking and not a joint action. The point can again be put in terms of the propriety of certain descriptions: the man who continues to put his rubbish in the bin when everybody else ceases to care is indeed putting his rubbish in the bin and keeping the yard tidier that it would be otherwise (he might even go so far as to collect everybody else's rubbish and put that in the bin, too), but he is not co-operating because he is no longer *helping* to keep the yard clean.

Some sort of joint or corporate activity, then, is required for a case of co-operation, but that must be more than a matter of each contributing to the production of the good. If each of us grows enough food to keep himself healthy then each of us contributes to the feeding of the population, but it does not follow that we are co-operating. Insofar as success in the feeding of the population is simply a summing of each man's success in feeding himself, the situation is just like that of the hikers and is not co-operative at all.

Nor is ruling out of the summing effect enough to create a co-operative situation. Professional entertainment, by and large, depends on money gathered from paying spectators. If there were no paying spectators then there would be no professional entertainment, but the effect is not merely one of summing, as it was in the case of feeding the population. That is, it is not the case that with one paying spectator we shall have a little entertainment, with two a little more (or a little better), and so on. Unless there are a fair number of paying spectators, professional entertainment will not get off the ground; support from a number of people is required.

Nevertheless, while those of us attending a performance might co-operate in a number of ways, we do not co-operate simply in attending the performance. The attendance of all of us, or suitable substitutes, is required if any one of us is to gain the good he seeks, but anybody who cannot afford a ticket or who would rather do his own painting at home or who simply does not enjoy the sort of performance in question, and who stays away without paying for a ticket, is not failing or refusing to co-operate. Each of us attends seeking only his own good and each of us depends for the attaining of that good on others acting similarly, but the activity is not co-operative.

If we saw ourselves as supporting the cause and doing our bit rather than simply seeking to enjoy ourselves by attendance at the performance, then we might be seen as co-operating. Something such as the preservation of the theatre we might all aim at, and we might all do our bit towards it. My taking pleasure in the performance is not, as the story was set out, something that we all aim at or try to bring about by our attendance. I aim at my pleasure by attending, but the rest of the audience may not know me from Adam.

Joint production of the particular good need not be aimed at for there to be co-operation. Assembly line workers putting together parts for a hydrogen bomb might not have the faintest idea what they are doing beyond putting flap A into slot B; they may have been told simply that it was important that they put flap A into slot B and that national security precluded their being told more. If each, for the good of either his country or his bank-balance, takes on his tiny part of the larger job, then each is co-operating with the others. They are co-operating even if each abhors and would refuse knowingly to work on a hydrogen bomb, having taken on this job only because he thought he was making parts for a better rat-trap as a defensive measure against biological warfare. It is clear that they are co-operating, despite their ignorance of the outcome, because each willingly and knowingly takes on a particular job as a job that meshes with others as part of a greater whole.

Nor is knowledge of the good that will be produced sufficient to make an activity co-operative. We may all be aware that as a result of competitive entry to the public service we gain a well-ordered society, but the competitors for posts are still competing and not co-operating. Each plays his part, a part without which the good would not be produced, and each knows that he is playing that part, but they are not co-operating.

It seems clear, then, that co-operation involves taking on a role or job as part of a larger job which others help to perform, the point of all these smaller, particular jobs being a contribution to the production of some good. The case must be describable in terms of such contribution to the production of a good, though it may also be described in other ways. As was suggested by considerations of hydrogen bombs and professional entertainments, whether they are co-operating depends on whether they take on the job or role as a contribution to a larger one, and not merely on whether certain results do follow on their activities.

Accepting a job as a contribution towards the achievement of a larger aim is not sufficient to make an activity co-operative, though it goes a long way towards doing so. That requirement by itself is not sufficient to rule out cases of exploitation or coercion. As one of several whom a violent robber attacks in order to support his family I co-operate neither with him nor with his other victims. There is no common aim in such a case recognised as limiting the activities of all the participants, defining their roles or jobs and thereby making them liable to claims. When we co-operate, each of us is part of a larger whole. The limitations imposed in terms of the activity are mutual, and each of us can make claims on the others even if the claims that a labourer can make on his foreman are not the same as those his foreman can make on him. This mutual limitation, the fact that each can make claims (that others should do their jobs) and that each is liable to claims (that he should do his own job) is at the core of co-operation and marks it off from cases of exploitation and coercion.

That claims can be made in this way is central to co-operative endeavour. In a co-operative enterprise one has responsibilities; one lets others down and is responsible for the failure if one fails to do the job. Proving that I was two miles away may prove that I am not responsible for your broken window, but a policeman assigned to points duty does not show that he cannot be held responsible for the traffic jam by proving that he was quietly drinking in a bar on the other side of town at the relevant time. If each person in an apartment block puts his rubbish in the bin instead of throwing it in the yard, then together they keep the yard clean, but they are acting independently, not co-operating, as long as they do not recognise that each has a claim on the others in this respect and would do wrong if he took to throwing his rubbish in the yard. This recognition of mutual claims and responsibility for a job is necessary for co-operation. Absence of these notions would rule out some apparent cases of co-operation, including, probably, most of those involving non-humans.

That co-operation involves having limitations placed on all participants rather than limitations placed on others by an unlimited few does not mean that all those involved in the enterprise have the same job so that there can be no distinction drawn between bosses and workers. In order to achieve some aim, a lot of different jobs may need to be done; some may grow food and others cook it, some may work out ways to produce more food and others work out the most efficient allocation of what we have, some may perform physical labour and others organise the performance of physical labour, and other still may work at checking to see that everybody is doing his job properly. Some people may be better at one sort of job than at another. But each person has his job, which he can do or fail to do, and, within the enterprise, performance of that job can be required of him. Some may make the decisions and others carry them out, but each has claims that he can make within the enterprise, including such claims as that he be paid a wage or otherwise share in the benefits produced by the activity.

The idea of jobs or roles, the claims that go with them and the rules that determine them, is essential to co-operation and is what marks that off from invisible hand cases, coercion, and so on. The rule is a constituent of the situation, and one without which the enterprise would not be co-operative; it is not something independent of the situation which is used simply as a standard against which to judge the activity. Without that rule the activity would not be what it is; the two are not independent of each other as the wrongness of kicking babies for fun is independent of people's acceptance or rejection of the rule that one ought not to kick babies for fun. If everybody rejects the rule that we ought not to kick babies, everybody can be wrong. If everybody rejects a rule which is a constituent of a co-operative enterprise, they neither are wrong nor do wrong; they simply have no co-operative enterprise of that nature.

An activity involving several people need not be either simply co-operative or simply non-co-operative; it can be co-operative to greater or lesser degrees. The point of any co-operative enterprise is the production of some good. That point, or the common aim of the enterprise, properly informs the organisation and the rules allocating jobs and claims. Insofar as the rules fail to correspond with that point, the activity becomes more coercive and pointless and less co-operative. Requirements that somebody bear burdens unnecessary for the carrying out of the enterprise make that enterprise less co-operative. (A requirement is something which can be claimed of him as he can make claims of others within the enterprise.) A group of us may decide to co-operate in the production of ball-bearings and distribute the jobs initially in terms of our interests and abilities. When the manager or inspector announces that nobody will be considered for promotion unless they put their spare time into doing his shopping for him, the joint activity becomes less co-operative. The requirement that he is making does not fit into the rationale of the co-operative activity. In general, as we might expect from the contrast between co-operation and exploitation, as relations between two participants in an endeavour become more unjust they become less co-operative.

Co-operative enterprises need not be discrete. There commonly is interplay between them, and sometimes conflict. We may all co-operate in a variety of ways by the payment of our taxes, but some may co-operate in a search for tax loopholes and a robber band may co-operate in a search for unearned income. The fact that people can co-operate in several different activities at once, and that there may be interplay between those activities, complicates the claims that can be made. Participation in one co-operative enterprise, such as a state organised to settle disputes by legal procedures, may generate a claim that I refuse to participate at all in some other co-operative enterprise, such as a robber band.

Not all co-operative enterprises are on a par. Some are more basic than others and presupposed by them, as the existence of a robber band is parasitic on the existence of other people on whom the robbers can prey. This does not mean that robber bands are parasitic on states or that the edicts of the state must always be accepted; bands of political revolutionaries are logically parasitic on the existence of the state, but sometimes the right thing to do might be to join the revolutionaries. Bands of robbers, bands of revolutionaries, and the state are all dependent on social life, and I shall argue later that social life is dependent on our co-operating with respect to basic decision-procedures for adjudication of disputes and alloca-tion of claims and sacrifices. The most basic of those decision-procedures, I shall argue, is our operation of the concept of justice. That is more basic than the state or any other particular organisation; it is called on to explain the authority of the state and how obligations can be generated by membership of other organisations.

Justice does not require that we co-operate in those very basic ways; it springs from that co-operation and informs it. That we co-operate in those ways is not forced on us by justice, but is a presupposition of social life. Once we recognise that and the role played in co-operation by the concept of justice, we can be clear how properly to set about adjudicating between competing claims generated by different co-operative enterprises, such as the state and a robber band, and how we can judge that some co-operative enterprises are simply improper. Argument about these points, however, must wait until later.

Moral practices, then, are co-operative practices and therefore involve claims. Because they are co-operative, they give the concept of justice a foothold and can thereby generate obligations of justice. This is what makes a practice into a moral practice. Moral practices are conceptually dependent on the notion of justice, and to understand them and the claims that they generate requires an account of the notion of justice.

This problem is one to which we shall proceed in due course. The nature and significance of moral practices, then, can be explained only in terms of a prior concept of justice. Practices cannot themselves be morally basic, but must arise and operate in terms of an independent morality. Because moral practices are so related to justice, the fact that a practice was itself unjust, as is slavery, would weaken the obligations that it generated; the practices are not independent of, but arise from and depend on, the prior morality. If a practice were sufficiently unjust, it would fail to generate any obligations at all.

The development of a practice cannot change what is otherwise unjust into what is just. The fact that a bunch of professional killers decided to co-operate in their tasks would not mean that killing was permissible for them or that one of them did wrong if he repented his ways and turned Queen's evidence rather than carry out the next killing when his turn came up, though the co-operative structure of the situation helps to explain why his fellow killers would regard him as having done wrong, as having failed to do his share, and as having betrayed them. The fact they are co-operating, if it is taken in isolation, does produce an obligation for the killer to take his turn, but what they are co-operating for is so unjust as to overrule completely that obligation when their activities are put in context instead of being taken in isolation.

The fact that I made a promise to do something is always relevant to whether or not I ought to do that something. It gives some reason of justice for my doing it, and, other things being equal, means that I ought to do it. Other things may not be equal, though, and may provide countervailing reasons. The man who leaves a maiden tied to the railway track simply because he has promised to meet Bertha elsewhere in five minutes shows no appreciation of the moral considerations which should be involved in promise-keeping as a moral activity. The man who promises to murder and then considers himself bound to do so shows a similar lack of appreciation. The fact that a promise has been made is still not irrelevant. When I find the maid tied to the railway track I ought to consider, even if I need not do so for long, my promise to Bertha, at least insofar as that I ought to explain and, perhaps, apologise to her later, and when the intervening factor is less serious I may have to consider the promise at greater length.

The man who promises to do something improper and the man who accepts that promise are both misusing the institution of promising. Promising can generate obligations only because of its place in a wider morality, and the point of co-operation with respect to the institution of promising is to facilitate arrangements within that wider context; to direct the institution against that context is to misuse it and undercut what is necessary to make that promise binding. (We might here compare the co-operative killers mentioned above.) One cannot properly at the same time deny what is necessary to make promises binding and insist that a promise binds. Such an inconsistency at least seems to mean that there is not even a vestigial obligation when somebody goes through the motions of promising about something he knows to be wrong, in which case he would not have succeeded in making a promise at all. The wrongness of his act, if he is unaware of it, displays no particular virtue or vice in him, but discovery of that fact between promise and fulfilment probably puts fulfilment in the same position as if the wrongness had been known in the first place. Unless the promisee had extracted the promise knowing it to be evil, the promiser is probably bound to do what he can towards substituting for the keeping of the immoral promise the nearest equivalent that is morally permissible.

Promises can, in that sort of way, take on a new significance after they have been made. Another way is by turning out to involve a much greater sacrifice than might reasonably have been expected when the promise was made. You might have promised to come to my house on Friday night and demonstrate some new woodworking technique. A freak storm might mean that, to keep your promise, you would have to walk three miles through knee-deep snow and ford a fast-flowing flooded river. In those circumstances, it would show a remarkable lack of concern for your interests if I insisted that you keep your promise. It would be grossly unfair of me to insist that you bear such a burden in order to give me some benefit, especially when the only burden I have borne is to avoid making engagements to play cards that night. But the unfairness of my insisting you should keep your promise means that the claims of justice that can be made on you in terms of your promise are weaker. You made a promise, and that fact has to be considered, but the unexpected and severe change in the relationship between benefits and burdens is also plainly relevant. We co-operate with respect to promising, and promising draws its bindingness from that co-operation, but co-operation is a matter of distributing benefits and burdens so that a severe re-distribution is a factor which must be considered. The promise is not wiped out or made invalid, but it may be over-ruled.

The mutuality of claims and the recognition as binding of a rule or established way of doing things is essential to co-operation and the generation of obligations. As the general recognition of claims weakens, so do the claims, until eventually the particular co-operative enterprise ceases to exist at all. When others cease to bear their burdens, I am not under an obligation to keep mine any more than I am under an obligation to keep a contract that the other party has broken. The point is not that one should meet claims only when it is immediately in one's interests to do so, but that the condition of reciprocity has been lost. Co-operation generates the claims. If people by and large do not recognise the claims, then there ceases to be co-operation. If there is no co-operation, then no claims can be made on me.

We might co-operate by not walking on the grass because we want a lawn. No one of us preserves the lawn by not walking on the grass; a much more general abstinence is required. On the other hand, no one of us will destroy the lawn by walking on the grass. If it is more convenient to walk across the lawn than to go the long way around to the bus stop, so that each of us has a burden to bear in keeping off the grass, then somebody might eventually take to slipping unobtrusively across the lawn rather than making the longer trip. After all, his doing that does not damage the lawn. Then another might follow his example, and another, and so on until the lawn cannot survive. At first I should be doing the right thing in not walking across the lawn, but at a later stage it would be foolish of me so to inconvenience myself. I am not getting the benefit of having a lawn anyway; the co-operation cannot achieve its point because so many of the others who were supposed to co-operate have not done so. The co-operation has collapsed, and, with it, the claims that could be made on me. I am under no obligation to walk around the patch of mud while others go straight across the middle.

As a different point, my refusing to walk across the mud and being righteous about it might help me to persuade others to return to the path of virtue which goes the long way round to the bus stop, but that is not a case of my meeting an obligation. The virtue to which I lead them is that of prudence in setting up (again) a co-operative enterprise to provide us with something we all want, and my righteous display is simply a ploy. No one person who walked on the grass destroyed it, but no one person had a right that the others lacked.

The same holds true of other cases in which co-operation collapses, though sometimes more complicatedly. If nobody else keeps his promises, then nobody can make any legitimate claim on me that I keep mine, and if no claim can be made on me then I have not made a promise. Once more, my doing what I 'promise' to do and being righteous about it might be a useful ploy in setting the institution up again. The situation with respect to promising is more complicated than with respect to public lawns, because one does not need such widespread co-operation. If the world should go to the dogs to such an extent that there were only two of us who paid any attention to promises, then the pair of us could still make promises to each other, and, if we made them, then we ought to keep them.

We can understand all this only if we put practices in their proper context of the rest of morality. The situation that Phillips and Mounce[2] ask us to consider is, therefore, an impossible one. They write:

Let us consider a people who have the practice of promise-keeping, and let us suppose that it is their sole moral practice. These people use the word 'ought' in what we should call a moral sense only in connection with the keeping of promises. Thus children are taught to do whatever they have undertaken to do, and sometimes to remind people who have not kept their word that they *ought* to do so. Their use of 'ought' is confined to this kind of circumstance. This practice of promise-keeping is therefore comparable with our own, except that we are to imagine it as being self-contained, as being isolated from any other moral practice.

In fact, this practice and the way it is developed in children are more readily comparable with such practices of ours as cleaning teeth after a meal or reading from the top left-hand corner of a page to the bottom right.

As is suggested by the claim that this is to be the only use of the word 'ought', Phillips and Mounce imagine this, not simply to be the sole moral practice, but the whole of morality in that society. It follows from my argument, though, that it would be impossible to have a society in which the relationship expressed by the word 'ought' arose only in those circumstances.

Phillips and Mounce deal with the matter as though it were impossible for the people in their society to ask why they should keep their promises, let alone to be given an answer. In that case, what marks this practice off from others as moral? Without being given reasons why one ought to keep one's promises there is nothing to mark this off from other practices as moral except for the fact that we all know what promising is and what moral significance it has within the context in which it actually occurs, which is one of a wider morality. In asking us to imagine that the practice and its significance remain when the rest of the context is removed, Phillips and Mounce ask us for more than they realise. The 'ought' in their imagined society would not have even the strength of the 'ought' in 'You ought to tip your hat to a lady', because that 'ought' does tie with a moral reason for acting; one can be insulting, inconsiderate, offensive, and so on by being discourteous. There may be no claim of reason in that rule of courtesy taken by itself, but it can develop a claim on us insofar as it fits into a wider context of morality and relationships with people. That rules of courtesy prescribe things to do and ways of doing them in order conventionally or symbolically to show respect allows things such as tipping one's hat or shaking hands to take on a new significance and to amount to something they would not otherwise have amounted to. But promising in the Phillips and Mounce society cannot have even that significance, because such a context is ruled out *ex hypothesi*.

Without 'ought' leading back to reasons and an answer to the question 'Why ought I?', Phillips and Mounce have described no proper use of 'ought' at all, let alone a moral use.

There must be an answer to the question 'Why ought I to keep my promises?' or there would be no connection between the practice of promising and practical reason. Reasons must come to an end somewhere, but not there and not just like that. Reasons lead us back to justice and the rest of morality.

NOTES

1 I have in mind particularly John Rawls, 'Two Concepts of Rules' (*Philosophical Review*, 1955) and 'Justice as Fairness' (*Philosophical Review*, 1958), and D.Z. Phillips and H.O. Mounce, *Moral Practices* (Routledge and Kegan Paul, London, 1970).
2 *Op. cit.*, p.11.

FOUR
Justice

In order to make clear the problem with which I am dealing, it is necessary to draw an often-drawn distinction: that between judicial and non-judicial justice, as it is sometimes called, or between the justice of an application of a law and the justice of a law. A law is applied justly if it is applied as a law and if the judge does not allow the fact that one of the litigants is his brother-in-law to affect his decision one way or the other: making an exception to a law is failing to apply that law, not applying it in a special way. Judicial justice has been done, or the law has been applied justly, if the judge considers all and only the legally relevant facts and applies the law to them correctly.

That is one fairly uncontentious sort of justice, but, at least on the face of it, there is another important sort: we can not only apply laws justly or unjustly, but can also assess those laws themselves as being just or unjust. This is an example of what is called non-judicial justice, and its distinctness from judicial justice might be brought out by considering a case that involves injustices of both sorts. Laws in South Africa prohibiting people of certain races from doing certain sorts of things might well be considered unjust, but an additional injustice would have been done if a judge, for personal reasons, prevented somebody from doing something by falsely classifying him as being of a race prohibited from that activity. In such a case we have not only an unjust law, but also an unjust application of a law; we have both a judicial and a non-judicial injustice.

Many philosophers have denied that there is any proper concept of non-judicial justice. Perelman[1], for example, denies that we can make any sense of describing a law as just or unjust except insofar as we are treating that law as being a more particular application of a more general law and employing the concept of judicial justice. The main motive behind philosophers' making this claim has been despair

71

consequent upon unsuccessful attempts to give an account of non-judicial justice. What I want to do in this section is to give the beginnings of such an account.

Justice is a concept which has application only in terms of a community or a group of people and makes no sense if applied to somebody considered completely in isolation from everybody else. There is a sense in which all moral concepts are social and arise from or take their point from relations between people, but justice is concerned with relations between people in a stronger way than that. If a man were marooned on a desert island and left all by himself with no chance of ever seeing anybody else again, his actions might be described as prudent or imprudent even in the older sense in which prudence is a virtue, as judicious or injudicious, or, at least at first blush, as right or wrong. One can, for example, imagine such a man giving serious thought to the propriety of suicide if his circumstances were particularly bad. But his actions could not be described as unjust because there is no group of people amongst whom benefits and burdens are to be distributed. With only one person there can be no question about alternative distributions of whatever is to be distributed, and insofar as there can be no question about alternative distributions there can be no question about the right or just distribution. Justice distributes burdens and benefits, including the artificial burdens of punishments for infractions of co-operative rules since those punishments may be necessary to re-establish the balance of burdens or to make co-operation worthwhile or possible for those who would not break the rules. Because it is a distributive concept, justice is applicable only in terms of a community or a group of people who are somehow interacting with each other.

This point, which is really quite obvious, is of some significance if we go on to ask the question: why is the concept of justice important? What is the point of the concept of justice that brings under it the variety of empirical elements that came under it? And the variety of empirical elements that can be brought under the concept of justice is enormous, the same empirical element being sometimes relevant and sometimes not. At least arguably, refusing a man a university post simply because he has a white skin is unjust but refusing him the part of Othello because he has a white skin is not; refusing a man a university post simply because he is a man is unjust, but refusing him the part of Desdemona on the same ground is not; that somebody is rich or poor is irrelevant to whether he ought to be refused an education but not irrelevant to how much he ought to be taxed; that he has committed a crime is irrelevant to whether his hospitalisation should be paid for from public funds but not to whether he ought to be fined or imprisoned; and so on.

No account of justice can be given if what is required is exhaustive lists of those empirical elements that come under it and those that do not, because the same elements would be on both lists and discrimination between the just and the unjust would therefore still be impossible. An account of justice, to be of any help, will have to explain why those empirical elements come under the concept when they do. When we see the point of considering those elements, what informs the concept of justice, then we can set about discriminating between the just and unjust interestingly because we shall know what sort of things to look for in the difficult cases. What the job of the concept is, or what its function is in our lives, determines what tools it has to call upon in the way of empirical elements. The questions 'What is this concept?' and 'Why is this concept as it is?' cannot be answered separately. With a mere list of the empirical elements coming under a concept and no account of why they come under it we have nothing like a guarantee that the list is exhaustive or that those elements are always relevant, and we do not know how to make inferences from the empirical elements to the application of the concept.

It is not simply a surprising fact about the world that people live in communities; it is something thrust upon us by our natures. I am not for the moment concerned with arguments about the necessity of a community for language and the necessity of language for rationality, but with empirical, everyday facts about the ways in which people are dependent upon each other. It is the needs and wants that we have in fact and the way the world is in fact that determine the problems we face and the concepts we have to develop in order to deal with them. It is the problems of satisfying our needs and wants in the world as it is, that gives point to or inform the concepts that we develop. It is not a matter of logical necessity that people are so vulnerable as to suffer sometimes in ways that make sympathy and special sorts of care appropriate, but, even as a quite unnecessary fact, that still gives point to our concept of illness.

Other facts about the way we are help to explain the point of the concept of justice. No one of us can provide for himself entirely, so the continuance of the human race requires and therefore presupposes some sort of social intercourse and co-operation with people helping each other. Unlike a new-born White Death shark, a new-born human being is not capable of looking after itself and providing itself with what is necessary if it is to live; facts such as this require some sort of community, even if not the present Western organisation of the family, if life is to continue. Even adults, in their prime and childless, who might not depend on a community to keep them alive, have much to gain from living in a community. Many things which no man could achieve by himself can be achieved by co-operative enterprise: around the clock defence against aggression, insurance schemes or some sort of guarantee that one will not starve when too old to work, the pooling and passing on of knowledge, and so on.

Morality has to do with the proper regulation of this social intercourse or communal life, and justice has to do with the proper distribution of benefits and burdens in the society and its co-operative enterprises. Each of us may benefit from joining in the communal life, but each us also, however willingly, thereby takes on certain burdens in the form of limitations on our freedom of action. If we are to have communal life then we need a way of resolving disputes, of dealing with those cases where interests come into conflict. Though we be ever so good-willed about clashes of interest, we shall need a way of settling them; our good will may mean that we will look for a way of resolving the problem and may even mean that we will find a way, but that is not the same thing as its being a way. Whether the problem be resolved by reference to a third party or by discussion between the two, there must be a way of working out the problem of apportioning whatever is in question if the communal life is to continue.

It may not be necessarily true that people's interests and desires clash, but it is as a matter of fact true, and it is such matters of fact that inform our concepts. As a matter of fact our interests sometimes clash, and as a matter of fact we sometimes clash about our interests. As a matter of fact we sometimes disagree about what to do when we must choose between courses of action, and we sometimes disagree about who will get what share of the goods or who must perform what share of the work. If we never disagreed about such things, that could be only because we agreed about the way of sorting them out and the solution in each case that came up and because each of us willingly limited himself to fit in with this solution each time. If we are to have communal life, that way of resolving disputes and of allocating benefits and burdens must be there; that is the way we are and the world is. In a world in which people must work to gain limited supplies of what we need or want, there are always questions about the distribution of benefits and burdens. That set of problems is what gives a point to or informs the concept of justice.

Many different accounts of distributive justice have been suggested: it has been said that a just distribution is one in which everybody has an equal share; that it is one in which the share that each person has is directly proportional to his need; that it is one in which the share that each person has is directly proportional to his merit; and so on. Any such account of justice I shall characterise as a positive account; an account of justice such as that given by Hobbes, according to which justice is no more and no less than the absence of injustice, I shall characterise as a negative account. I want to argue now that the concept of injustice is primary, so that any satisfactory account of justice must be a negative account. I shall argue for this conclusion by introducing the principle of plenitude.

A good exists in plenitude when there is so much of it that, no matter how much of it one person takes, there is more than enough left to satisfy the wants and needs of all other people. An example of this would be the position with respect to air in normal circumstances, and contrasted with it might be what seems to be the position in the world today with respect to food. The contrast could be set up in this way: in the case of food, where there is not enough to go around, any food that somebody takes he takes at the expense of somebody else; on the other hand, with more than enough air to go around, somebody who takes air does not do so at the expense of somebody else. In the one case, satisfying one person's wants and needs means depriving another; in the other case it does not. So, with unlimited air, we are not faced with a case of injustice when one person takes more air than anybody else simply because he feels like doing deep-breathing exercises. When one person takes more food than anybody else simply because he wants to experience the bloated feeling that follows a big meal, we may well be faced with a case of injustice.

That is what it is for a good to exist in plenitude. The principle of plenitude, though, requires access as well as existence in plenitude; the principle of plenitude is satisfied if the good is obtainable in plenitude to everybody. If, for example, air exists in plenitude, then it satisfies the principle of plenitude if nobody is being throttled and if no other condition obtains which would prevent anybody from gaining air in plenitude. The principle of plenitude is satisfied if a good exists in plenitude and if it is available in plenitude to everybody, i.e. if nobody is deprived of having that good in the amount in which he wants it either by other people's taking the good or by having his access to it blocked by anything within the control of human beings or institutions. (The qualification 'within the control of human beings or institutions' should really be omitted in discussing the principle of plenitude because justice is a practical concept the point of which is to guide possible activities, and if nothing could be done to change a distribution then that distribution would not be unjust.) I think that the principle of plenitude provides us with an interesting case when we are considering justice.

One thing that the principle of plenitude makes clear is that no general account of justice can be given in terms of equality, though considerations of justice might require an equal distribution in certain circumstances. It should be clear that in a case in which the principle of plenitude is satisfied no injustice is done no matter what the distribution be, and I shall try to show that, in these cases, it follows from the lack of injustice that any distribution is just. If X satisfies the principle of plenitude, then no matter how much of X I may take I shall do no injustice to you.

Nor does justice require simply that the distribution be one in accordance with needs: if one person, or everybody, takes more than his needs would require, no injustice is done so long as the principle of plenitude is satisfied. It should be noted at this stage, though, that the principle of plenitude has built into it the minimum condition that everybody's needs be satisfied or satisfiable at his will. The principle of plenitude is satisfied only if there is so much of some good and only if access to it is such that, no matter how much anybody takes, everybody else can still satisfy his wants and needs.

It should be clear that no matter what *positive* criterion is suggested for justice, the same point can be made. Any positive criterion for justice, such as that justice is what is required by needs or by any other characteristic, will be such as to require some particular distribution in any given case. But when the principle of plenitude is satisfied, justice is done no matter what the distribution be, so no positive account of justice can be satisfactory.

Some philosophers would no doubt say that the principle of plenitude cannot be used to make these points[2] because, when the principle of plenitude is satisfied, questions of justice cannot be raised; a good that satisfies the principle of plenitude is distributed neither justly nor unjustly. To say that it was distributed either justly or unjustly, they would say, would be to talk nonsense: 'just' and 'unjust' are not logical opposites like 'red' and 'not-red'. According to the law of excluded middle everything is either red or not-red, so that pillar-boxes are red and the concept *hexagonal* is not-red. Similarly, everything will be either just or not-just, but it does not follow that everything will be either just or unjust any more than that everything will be red or blue. Without an unusual explanatory story it makes no sense to point at a stone or a speck of dust and say 'That is just' or 'That is unjust'. There are some things of which it makes no sense to predicate justice.

Nevertheless, I am unsympathetic to the view that questions of justice cannot be raised about a good that satisfies the principle of plenitude, because (1) distribution is most certainly not one of the things of which it makes no sense to predicate justice, (2) the question is one of distribution, and (3) it is not a necessary truth of any good that it satisfies the principle of plenitude.

To say 'This satisfies the principle of plenitude; is it just?' may indeed be to say something logically unusual, but to ask of X (when X does, as a matter of fact, satisfy the principle of plenitude) 'Is the distribution of X just?' is not to ask a nonsensical question. If a new gas has been discovered, then the question 'Is it coloured?' is a perfectly meaningful and sensible question. If I know that the gas is green, the question is still meaningful, though, in many circumstances, for me to ask it would be silly.

It is not a necessary truth of any good that it satisfies the principle of plenitude. If air exists in plenitude, the principle of plenitude still may not be satisfied: somebody may be being throttled, or the incident of the Black Hole of Calcutta may be repeated, and either of these would result in, amongst other things, an unjust distribution of air. The fact that these phenomena result in an unjust distribution of air may or may not be the most important moral point, but it is one moral feature of the situation. To determine that something satisfies the principle of plenitude we must ensure there is no deprivation of this sort, and in so doing we are raising and answering a question of justice. The question 'It satisfies the principle of plenitude; is it distributed justly?' is an odd question in just the same way as 'It is green: is it coloured?'. But to ask of X, when X does as a matter of fact satisfy the principle of plenitude, 'Is X distributed justly?' is to ask a perfectly proper question.

In this context, we might consider some of the arguments about air polution as arguments that the principle of plenitude is ceasing to be satisfied with respect to air. Considering the arguments in that light might help to make the point that it is not a necessary truth that any good satisfies the principle of plenitude and to show the significance of that point. Air is necessary for us, and even if it satisfies, or used to satisfy, the principle of plenitude, people can so act as to change the world in ways that would mean that air no longer satisfied the principle. Because air is necessary for us, the possibility of people's acting in that way is important and needs to be checked. There is always an issue of justice about the availability of air to people; that issue is resolved, not ruled out, by a demonstration that air still satisfies the principle of plenitude.

So questions of justice can properly be raised about goods that satisfy the principle of plenitude, and I tried to show earlier that one consequence of this is that no positive account of justice can be satisfactory. Justice is negative; the concept of justice serves to rule things out from being done rather than to prescribe some particular thing as what ought to be done, even if, as conditions normally stand, it does not effectively limit us to one thing that may be done. That fact arises from the nature of the conditions rather than from the concept of justice. No positive account of justice can be satisfactory, so justice is to do, not with the *possession* of certain characteristics, but with the *lack* of certain characteristics, and in particular to do with the lack of deprivation of certain sorts. (Note that, as I am using the term, being deprived of something is not the same as simply not having enough; if I am to be deprived of X then it must be the case that, by the activity of human beings and institutions, I could be provided with enough, even if that meant that other people did not have enough.) What we need, then is an account of injustice. Once we have that, we need say only that anything about which questions of justice can be raised is just if it is not unjust.

The account of justice that I want to give, then, is a negative one: justice consists simply in the absence of injustice. Justice is done when all accusations of injustice can be rebutted. This negative approach to justice has several advantages. As I shall try to show, it leaves room for the manoeuvres of cross–categorial arguments, which is an essential feature of any satisfactory account of justice. It also allows a satisfactory solution to the main problem that I have raised so far in this chapter. I have argued that the possibility of a good's satisfying the principle of plenitude constitutes an objection to any positive account of justice: when the principle of plenitude is satisfied, any distribution is just. Hence, when the principle of plenitude is satisfied, justice does not require that the distribution be in accordance with needs, merits, or any other criterion that might be suggested in a positive account of justice. It seems that the only sort of account of justice that will cover such a case is the negative account: the claim that justice is done when all accusations of injustice can be rebutted. When the principle of plenitude is satisfied, therefore, justice must be being done.

So much for justice. Injustice I define thus: an injustice is done when somebody is deprived of something in favour of somebody else and the deprivation cannot be justified by reference to essential categories or relevant characteristics. It should be noticed that this definition imposes two conditions, both of which must be satisfied for a case of injustice to exist. It is because both conditions must be satisfied that not all deprivations are injustices, and that not all distributions which cannot be justified by reference to essential categories are injustices. It is because of that that we can deal satisfactorily with the possibility of the principle of plenitude's being satisfied.

Now we have the quick definitions of justice and injustice, but clearly there is quite a bit yet to be done. In particular, the notion of an essential category needs to be discussed, and some attention needs to be paid to the problems of cross-categorial argument. I shall discuss the notion of an essential category first.

The notion of an essential category is taken over from Professor Perelman[3], who thinks that no sense can be made of the notion of non-judicial justice, but that justice is simply the application of a rule that must, ultimately, take its value from the other values at the base of the system within which it is a rule. Ultimately, he thinks, we simply choose our basic moral values and erect a system on those foundations; in this realm there can be no argument, and there can be no argument between two people who disagree in this way about whether or not a rule is a just rule. 'If we regard a rule as unjust because it accords pre-eminence to a different value, we can only note the disagreement. No reasoning will be able to show that one of the opponents is wrong'.[4]

Perelman, then, defines formal justice as '*a principle of action in accordance with which beings of one and the same essential category must be treated in the same way*'.[5] An essential category is a characteristic shared by a group of people and referred to in the rule so that it brings that group of people under the rule; what makes it an *essential* category is simply the fact that it is referred to in this rule.

To get concrete justice from this formula we simply fill in the essential category in some way. If we fill it in in terms of needs we get 'All people with the same needs must be treated in the same way'. If we fill it in in terms of merits we get 'All people with the same merits must be treated in the same way'. Formal justice is simply the form of a principle of concrete justice and can never prescribe an action because the essential category, be it needs, merit, or whatever else, is not specified. As an action can be prescribed only by a principle of concrete justice, so an action or distribution can be judged only by reference to a principle of concrete justice. Whenever the concept of justice is applied to some action or distribution, it is a principle of concrete justice that is being brought to bear.

In a sense, then, Perelman's account leads to the conclusion that there are several different concepts of justice: there is a concept of needs-justice, a concept of merit-justice, and so on, but there is no concept of simply-justice. That is why, if two people disagree about the justice of distribution D, one saying that it is just and the other saying that it is unjust, they need not be contradicting each other but may both be right; one of them may be speaking of needs-justice and the other of merit-justice, for example. The same action can be just in terms of needs and unjust in terms of merit.

The main problem raised by Perelman's account is that it allows only one characteristic to be considered in any case in which somebody is trying to work out a just distribution. 'The persons under consideration can be divided into two categories according as the sole characteristic taken into account is present or absent.'[6] As Perelman has defined justice, there is no possibility of working out a simply-just solution to a problem of distribution if the problem involves a crossing of categories; *either* merit *or* needs can be brought into the picture, but we cannot cross categories and consider both of them at once as we try to work out a just solution. If consideration in terms of needs would require that labourer L be paid a higher wage than worker W, and consideration in terms of work or merit would require that worker W be paid a higher wage than labourer L, then, according to Perelman, we can apply needs-justice or merit-justice to our problem, but there is no way of working out what is simply a just solution. Considering both categories at once would mean forsaking the requirements of either in reaching a compromise, and that would mean that the solution, failing to satisfy the requirements of needs-justice, merit-justice, or any other category, was in no way just.

On my account, a compromise solution need not fail to be just. In the case described above, for example, the accusation of injustice made by saying that the payments decided upon are not in accordance with the works of L and W would be rebutted by referring to their needs. This is, of course, only a crude outline; I shall try later on to give a more detailed account of some of the considerations that would have to be raised in settling a problem of this sort.

Injustices can arise from an incorrect choice of essential categories just as well as from any other cause: the choice of skin-colour or religion as an essential category frequently does result in injustice. One of the difficulties in Perelman's account of justice is that he allows anything at all to be an essential category in any circumstances, and I want to avoid this difficulty by giving some account of how essential categories are to be chosen.

One move that is often made at this stage of the game is to say that justice requires that in making a distribution we take heed only of morally relevant characteristics of the people concerned, i.e. to say that essential characteristics cover morally relevant characteristics of people. Such a move, though, would be circular. Morality stands as a determinable to the determinants justice, kindness, and so on, and what makes the characteristic morally relevant in this case is not something to do with benevolence or courage, but something to do with justice. If the problem is one of justice, then the characteristic concerned is relevant to morality in that it is relevant to justice, so in order to explain how it is morally relevant we should have to explain how it is relevant to a question of justice. That is the question from which we began, so the move gets us nowhere.

It might be suggested that the problem of relevance, or of what are to count as essential characteristics, should be treated only in a piecemeal way, and not generally, as I am trying to treat it. In the particular case, it might be said, it will be clear what is relevant and what is not: if people are being taxed, then the amount of money that they have will be a relevant consideration and the colour of their skins will not be; if people are being auditioned for the part of Hamlet, then acting ability will be a relevant consideration and skin colour may well be, but the amount of money that they have will not be. In the particular case, it might be said, there is no problem about what is relevant and what is not, but no general account can be given.

This account leaves a problem: if no general account of any sort can be given, then it is not clear how we should go about settling a dispute between two people who disagree about the relevance of some characteristic. It also leaves another problem: it presupposes certain things about the aim of what is being done in the particular case. If we could assume that those in charge of the particular case were operating with a sense of justice and were trying to achieve justice then all might be well, but we should be no further forward in giving an analysis of justice. The immoral tyrant who wants to consolidate his regime by distributing power and benefits only amongst his supporters has different aims, and he has chosen characteristics which are obviously relevant to the distribution in his case. More must be said than that relevance is clear in particular cases.

The concept of a need I intend to define in terms of the causal relation, thus: a need is something without which a certain goal cannot be achieved or a certain state reached or maintained, and the goal or state needs to be specified for clarity and completeness. Thus: 'It needs an extra pinch of salt' — to achieve that certain flavour; 'She needs a sea holiday' — to restore her health; 'I need three hands' — to get the packing done in time. Whether or not something is a need will depend on the context, or the aim in view. In many cases the normal standard of living in the society will be assumed, and by reference to it we might mark off certain things as luxuries: what is quite properly regarded in one society or at one time as a need may be regarded in another as a luxury. One way in which people may disagree about what is needed is by disagreeing about the goal in view. Another way is by disagreeing about what causes will bring about certain effects.

This is not meant to say that all needs are on a par and that the needs of a hostess in decorating her dinner table are as important as a starving man's need for food; it is not meant to deny that some needs are more basic than others. Needs can arise only under certain conditions; unless one is alive one cannot be a hostess and have needs to do with the decoration of a table and the delectation of guests, so the needs for such things as food to keep one alive are more basic than the needs one might have as a hostess. Some sort of rough and ready ranking of needs can no doubt be arranged in this way, though the job depends on consideration of the question of to whom or what one should be just. What is needed to attain a lower standard of living, we can say as a rough guide, will be more basic than what is needed to attain a higher standard of living. Basic needs, perhaps, are those needs which must be satisfied if a person is to have the standard of living that renders him properly capable of co-operation and not merely an object of exploitation, giving him a choice, so that he does not feel that he must simply take whatever is offered. Just what this standard of living is would probably vary with the standard of living of those with whom the person in question might co-operate. The notion of what is basic seems to be a comparative one.

Since the term 'standard of living' is commonly employed to refer to a standard of consumption within one particular way of life, this might at first glance seem to leave a problem about whether needs from different 'life-styles' are comparable. There is very little point in showing a sunset to a man who wants a motor car or giving a motor car to a man who wants to see a sunset, and it is perhaps not clear how the one man's yearning is comparable with that of the other. This same apparent difficulty, though, can arise even within one 'life-style' if we have to compare the needs of people who have different wants, but it seems somewhat clearer how we should compare a bridge-player's need for cards with a footballer's need for a ball. The point is covered in terms of the way in which some needs presuppose the satisfaction of other needs. All of us need food and drink. All of us in the relevant circumstances need heating to protect us against blizzards or a place to hide from tigers. Beyond that point we may well differ, and what I need in order to make me happy may be as different from what you need to make you happy as is what I need to cure my disease from what you need to cure yours. The needs can be made comparable by bringing them under common descriptions such as what people need to make them happy or what people need to restore their health. One man's need for a motor car is comparable with another man's need to see a sunset in that both are cases of a need for something in order to make somebody happy.

So, suppose I say that an essential category is a need.

My account would then be this: justice is done when all accusations of injustice can be rebutted, and an injustice is done when somebody is deprived of something and the distribution cannot be justified by reference to needs. But any simple identification of essential categories with needs leads to trouble.

People live in groups or societies, and questions of justice can be raised only if there is a group or society. This means that the milieu in which anybody is acting is one of other people, and that fact leads to difficulties if we simply identify essential categories with needs as I have accounted for needs. In some societies one needs to have a skin of a certain colour in order to be allowed to receive a formal education or certain other benefits. If any simple identification of essential categories with needs is made, that means that skin colour is an essential category, i.e. that distributional preferences justified only by reference to skin-colour are just. This is a conclusion that I should like to avoid.

It might well be objected here that we are trying to assess laws as just or unjust, and that we should therefore not allow the laws to be in any way judges in their own case: the problem posed above arises only because we allow an unjust law to determine needs and therefore to prejudice the issue of its own justice in its own favour. The problem is solved, it might be said, if we consider the situation as though there were no law requiring a white skin for education.

But this reply misconstrues the nature of the problem. Wherever there is mass prejudice against a minority group, there may well be co-operative enterprises carried out by the majority in which they refuse to allow members of the minority to join, and it might be the case that the minority is not large enough to run such an enterprise itself. It will then be the case that to join in the enterprise in question one would need certain things: one might need a white skin, one might need to be a Christian, or it might be something else. What raises the problem is not simply the presence of unjust laws, but the fact that when one is acting in a society what one can do depends partly on what other people do, partly on what they will help one to do, and partly on what they will prevent one from doing. The actions of other people can create needs in one.

One might point out that there could be no discrimination against people with black skins in a society completely made up of people with black skins, or no discrimination against Jews in a society completely made up of Jews, and try to introduce a test of the universalisability sort to limit the needs that can be considered relevant for the purposes of justice. Universalisability is a confused idea; objections to it are very well known, though some of them depend on a failure to distinguish between different sorts of universalisability. The idea must quickly go by the board here. In a society wholly made up of Jews, discrimination against Jews on the grounds of their Jewishness is impossible; if that means that non-Jewishness is not a need or essential category, then the same test precludes everything else's being a need or essential category. In a society in which all were equally strong, weakness could not give rise to needs relevant to justice. And so on.

Problems about Jewishness or black skins arise only because of beliefs that people hold about them, so the obvious thing to do is to rule out those beliefs from consideration. Can we say that needs should be assessed on the basis of a person's characteristics independently of what people believe about those characteristics? This would be to say that in the case of a co-operative enterprise we should consider only whether the people could co-operate and not merely whether they will co-operate: this would make it unjust to exclude a man from a health scheme on the basis of his Jewishness, because his Jewishness would not make co-operation impossible; what makes co-operation impossible are the beliefs that some people hold about Jewishness. It would not mean that it was unjust to exclude a Jew from membership in a delegation representing Baptist opinion to the local council: here it would be the Jewishness that gave rise to the difficulties, and not merely beliefs held about it.

An account of justice in terms of distribution and deprivation, such as I have been suggesting, must give to needs an important place, and, indeed, I want to give to needs a basic place in the account of justice. Why needs should have so important a place in the concept of justice should emerge from what was said earlier about the importance and function of the concept of justice. Morality has to do with the proper regulation of communal life and the co-operative enterprises into which we enter in communal life, and justice has to do with the proper distribution of benefits and burdens. I do not want to hang too much on this story, and I do not intend that it should, by itself, give us the concept of justice, but it does help us to understand the role of needs in justice: the point of entering into co-operative enterprises, of working and giving and taking, is to satisfy needs. The story helps to explain the rationale behind the concept. It does not prove anything, but it helps to explain why the concept is what it is and why the essential categories are what they are.

We saw in the previous section that there is a close connection between co-operation and justice, so close that the notion of co-operation cannot properly be understood without reference to the notion of justice. As relations between people become more unjust they become less co-operative, turning rather into the coercive or exploitative. It is in terms of justice that we distinguish co-operation from exploitation, and thus it is in terms of justice that we make our proper claims upon each other within a co-operative enterprise.

The relationship of dependence between co-operation and justice, though, does not run in only one direction; the home of justice is in dealing with co-operation, and it is in terms of co-operation that justice must be understood. Its function, as was suggested earlier, is to regulate the distribution of benefits and burdens when people co-operate in communal life, each taking on a job, at least in the form of recognising some limitations on his activities, in order that all may benefit. The acceptance in co-operation of jobs that mesh with each other appears in justice as the mutal acceptance of burdens, and that the acceptance be mutual is just as much required as that co-operative jobs mesh; justice is a notion of reciprocity and will not make requirements of one person alone.

What justice requires of one person depends on how others behave. Our contract may require that you do A for me and that I do B for you, but justice does not require that I do B if you break the contract. Justice requires all sorts of things of one in a civilised life which it would not require of one in the Hobbesian war of each against all, where force and fraud may well be the primary virtues. In a civilised life it is unjust if one takes what is another's or does not act appropriately after saying 'I promise', but, if everybody else takes what he wills and recognises no distinction between mine and thine or refuses to place any significance on the words 'I promise', then justice does not require that one pay one's debts, return borrowed books, or keep one's promises. Nor does justice require in those circumstances that one keep money or books obtained from others or that one not do what one said one promised to do; where others will recognise no limitations, justice places no limitations on one and allows anything. If the claims are never recognised then there is no institution of property or promising, so repayment of debts and keeping of promises, far from being required, would be impossible; we could neither incur debts nor make promises. It would be unfair were one person so limited and the others not.

It might be kind, though neither just nor unjust, to return money dropped by a Hobbesian enemy; it is more likely to be simply foolish. The man who thinks that rules formulated to deal with one set of circumstances must apply also in quite different circumstances shows only moral confusion. Of course one must be just in the Hobbesian natural condition, but that requires no particular action, nothing *in foro externo*: in the Hobbesian natural condition justice allows anything because the others recognise no limitations. A reasonable belief that others will accept the limitations is a necessary condition for getting any co-operative enterprise off the ground, whether or not we have security in that belief only when it is backed by the sword. Without a reasonable belief that each of us would accept the limitations, it is not clear how we could make a contract, let alone break it.

Justice imposes requirements in related sets. If you keep your part of the contract then I must keep mine, and vice versa. If you accept the limitations on your behaviour to my advantage, then I must accept the limitations on my behaviour to your advantage. This co-operative mutual limitation assigns us our tasks in the enterprise; our claim to the advantages of others' being limited depends on our acceptance of the burden of limitation, and others' claims that we should accept the burden depend on their recognition of our claim to the advantages. The relatedness of sets of requirements imposed by justice expresses the way in which roles mesh in a co-operative enterprise.

This claim about the function of reciprocity in the operation of justice is a significant one, and its significance should not be misunderstood. The claim is not that it is not worthwhile to be just unless one gets something in return; it is, rather, that unless one gets something justice will not require that one gives something. It is not that it is not worthwhile to be just by giving somebody five dollars unless he has previously loaned one the money; unless he has, there can be no repayment of a debt, and justice does not require that one simply hand over five dollars. (There might, of course, be other reasons making it unjust not to give him the money.)

What one gets back in the case of justice need not be at all straightforward, and is best understood in terms of the mutual recognition of claims. Promises, unlike contracts, are usually one-sided and will give benefit (at least in the form of a right, which he might exercise to somebody else's material benefit) to the receiver of the promise. The maker of the promise need receive no benefit from making it, and the promise that he makes need not be paired with any other promise from which he benefits. And yet the breaking of a promise is wrong, I shall argue later, in that it is an injustice. What one gets, in the case of promising, and what acts as the basis on which a claim can be made, is the use of an institution which sometimes allows claims to be made against one and sometimes allows one to make claims. Again, it is a matter of reciprocity, but not a matter of whether it is worthwhile being just if one gets nothing for it. If enough other people fail to keep their promises, then what follows, very crudely, is not that it is not worthwhile for me to be just by keeping my promises, but that the institution withers away so that it generates no just claims at all and it is impossible for me to make, break, or keep promises. Reciprocity is required in the mutual recognition of claims.

The point of this reciprocity we have already seen: it is that justice has its home in co-operation, and co-operation gives members of the co-operative endeavour claims on each other. The requirement of reciprocity in justice is this mutual recognition of claims. If the claim ceases to be mutually recognised, then the co-operative endeavour simply ceases to exist, and, in that context, justice requires nothing because there is nothing on which it can get a purchase. One cannot be unjust in those circumstances because there are no just claims that one can refuse to recognise. An extreme Hobbesian natural condition of mankind is the same set of circumstances writ much larger: there are no co-operative relations at all between people, and no trust with each man's hand turned against every other. In such a condition, it would not follow that it was not worth anybody's while to be just. In the absence of any reciprocity or co-operative relations, it would rather follow that there were no just claims that one could refuse to meet and, therefore, that it was impossible for one to be unjust. In such a situation, justice would not prohibit any action at all. One ought still to be just, perhaps, but there would be no way of turning that into any specific sort of requirement about one's behaviour. And the reason for that is not that it would not be worth one's while to be just, but that it would be impossible to be unjust.

This is the context in which the concept of justice has its place, and it suggests a list of essential categories. The essential categories that I shall list are need, work, and merit, and the place of work and merit in the pattern should emerge if we consider needs in giving an account of them. Unless reference is made to needs it might be difficult to rule out somebody who wants to say, for example, that having a white skin is a merit. We might also find it difficult to sort out work from play: actions are performed and energy expended in either, and, to make the difficulty more apparent, there is a case for saying that professional sport is work and amateur sport play, the case resting not simply on the fact that professionals are paid but on such points as whether the rationale of the particular sporting event is one of pleasure for players or entertainment for spectators. Something must be done towards limiting what can count as merit or work. (Note that the story explaining why the concept of justice takes the form that it does also explains why needs should be discounted if they arise from aims which involve the disruption of communal life or are inconsistent with the idea of co-operative enterprise of which the person with the aim is a part.)

I want to suggest, then, that essential categories are needs or contributions to the satisfaction of needs within a context of co-operation. That is to say, an essential category is a characteristic which, independently of beliefs about it, is a need or contributes co-operatively to the amount of a good available for distribution. I suspect that the only three characteristics coming under this description are needs, works, and merit, but whether I am right about that is independent of this general account of what essential categories are.

A good is anything that satisfies a need consistent with communal life, so that both shirt buttons and amusement can be goods. Work, then, is limited to co-operative work producing or maintaining goods for the satisfaction of needs. The work must be co-operative, done within a context of mutual claims, else gratitude would never mean more than what we feel towards the grocer when we pay for his groceries and selfless help would be impossible; the distinction between a debt and a debt of gratitude would be lost. If the grocer says to forget his bill *then* we owe him a debt of gratitude, but there has been no change at all in the situation if a debt of gratitude is the same morally or legally enforceable sort of thing as the original debt.

Merit is perhaps best understood as a sort of potential work. Making a co-operative enterprise worthwhile sometimes involves taking out insurance even though the mishaps insured against might not occur. In the same way, people who made themselves available as, say, policemen, soldiers, or doctors would have a claim on the goods produced by the enterprise even though, in the absence of crime, war, disease, and injury they were never actually called upon to work. They may not, in fact, expend energy in the co-operative enterprise, but they fill roles in it and stand ready to work; they place themselves within the system of mutual claims so that work can be claimed of them when the occasion arises. Somebody who keeps himself outside that system of mutual claims and refuses to co-operate has no basis for a one-way claim to a share of the goods no matter how brave he is or how much he knows about medicine.

The word 'merit' is more commonly used in a different way, simply to refer to somebody's bravery, intelligence, or other virtues. We have seen, though, that co-operation and justice require a system of mutual claims, and such merits give a person no claim provided that he keeps himself outside that system. Such virtues are properly considered in co-operative enterprises, but they give rise to questions of efficiency rather than to questions of justice. It is much more efficient (and a proper ground for awarding jobs, given the point of the enterprise) if labouring jobs go to those who are strong, actuarial jobs to those who can calculate accurately, military jobs to those who are brave, and so on.

Consider, then, how objections of unjust deprivation might be met by reference to these categories.

If somebody objects that it is unfair that he should be given less of a good than somebody else, he is saying that he has been given less of that good than the other person and that there is no good reason why he should be given less. But he must have in mind a good reason of a particular sort. An immoral tyrant who wanted to consolidate support for his regime, as we have seen, might have good reason for arranging the distribution of goods in such a way that those who supported him got more than those who opposed him, but reference to a reason such as this would not show the distribution to be just. Also, showing that something is for the greatest good of the greatest number will not show it to be just though the minority be downtrodden: this is where arguments against Utilitarianism fit in. Reasons of a certain sort are needed, and I suggest that they are reasons to do with essential categories, i.e. reasons to do with characteristics related to needs in the ways described.

So, if one person objects that it is unfair that he should be given less of a good than another person, a reply pointing out that the other person has three infants and a disease-riddled wife to keep and therefore has greater needs would be a reply tending to show that the distribution was a just one. The whole point of the enterprise is the satisfaction of needs. This reply refers only to the category of needs, assuming it to be the only category relevant in the case.

But if X receives more of some good than does Y, Y might point out that he and X have the same needs and object that the distribution is therefore unjust. If the circumstances are right, it is possible to reply to this objection by reference to the categories of work or merit. It could be pointed out that X has done more than Y and has therefore provided more of the good for distribution by exceeding what could properly be required of him; that Y's basic needs are satisfied, that he has the share he would have had if X had not done the extra work, and that he has even benefited from the extra amount of the good produced by X's extra work (Y and the others in the enterprise would have some claim to a share in the extra goods because X's work producing extra goods was co-operative, not independent, and therefore depended on them; if X's work were independent and not in the co-operative enterprise, the question of their claims to a share in what he produced, say, working alone in his home at night after a full day in the factory, would not arise); and that there is, therefore, a clear sense in which, in giving X something extra for the extra work that he has done, one does not deprive Y: far from being deprived, Y has benefited from the extra work that X has been paid for doing.

Similarly, where X has done more work than Y but they have each been given the same amount of a good, an objection of unjust deprivation could be met if Y has greater basic needs than X and the surplus goods provided by X's work must be given to Y if his needs are to be satisfied. That Y's basic needs have not been satisfied really means that the enterprise as a whole must produce more, therefore increasing the claims which can properly be made on anybody in the enterprise. If the organisation is such that the extra burden has to fall on X because of the particular job that he has, then so be it. If the extra burden could have fallen on Y, then it should have fallen there. The greater the claims that he makes, the greater the claims that could be made on him. To require the extra work of X rather than Y in those circumstances would be unjust in the same way as our earlier case of the manager who announced that nobody would be considered for promotion unless they put their spare time into doing his shopping for him.

In the same sort of way, where X has done more work than Y but they have each been given the same amount of a good, an objection of unjust deprivation could be met by reference to merit, pointing out that Y held himself ready to deal with all victims of industrial accidents and it is simply a matter of fact that there were very few of them. Y was in a position where work could be claimed of him and he met all the claims that were made, so he can make the correlative claim to a share in the goods even though very few claims were in fact made of him. Because of the particularly arduous work for which he was making himself available and the fact that X benefited from his so making himself available, even though he had not had to act on this occasion, Y might even be able to claim a greater share than X and not merely the same. It is in this sort of way that cross-categorial arguments will work.

It should be noticed that giving an extra amount of some good for work or merit is severely limited by the justifying argument set out above. The argument requires that attention be paid to at least the minimum of needs all around, so that the person receiving less does in fact benefit from the work or merit of the person receiving more. Needs continue to play their basic part in the concept of justice.

There are, then, reasons why just shares need not be equal shares even when there is only a limited amount of a good available for distribution. Basic needs themselves will vary to some extent with the nature of the particular co-operative enterprise and the role that a man has in it. Basic needs will be not only such things as food and drink, but what a man needs of what is produced if he is to be able to enter the enterprise and do his job. In order to do his particular job, a man might need a typewriter, a tape-recorder, or a car. If they are necessary for him to play his part in the enterprise, then they are basic needs and count as part of his basic allotment; they do not, so to speak, come out of his share of the profits. It should be clear, though, that such entitlements on the ground of necessity are strictly cases of need and are not mere perks of office. The test is whether, independent of anybody's beliefs about the situation and what he is entitled to in it, the job could be done without the typewriter, tape-recorder, or car. For this sort of justification to work, it must be from the privileged person's privileges that the general benefits flow: they must not be independent of the benefits or they will have to be justified in some other way, such as by reference to work or merit. In the proper case of privilege we do not defend the choice of distribution (at least with respect to the privilege) but show that the distribution could not be otherwise if the enterprise is to be carried on at all. The advantages gained by the privileged person are part of the generally beneficial role that he plays and are inseparable from it. If the advantages are separable from the role he plays, then they stand in need of justification by reference to essential categories.

It should be clear that, while needs are basic, they are basic only within a system of justice. There may be circumstances in which a man has a proper claim to a share of the goods produced even though he has done no work, circumstances I have described as constituting cases of merit, but it does not follow that a man can refuse to do any work and can then properly insist, on grounds of justice, that at least his basic needs be satisfied. Such a man might be favoured by benevolence and fed by the kind, but, as he has refused the relationship of mutual claims with the others, justice favours him not at all and leaves him to fend for himself. (This assumes, of course, that he is not related to them in some other co-operative enterprise on which he bases his claim, and cases in which somebody has no co-operative relationship with others will be very rare.) Burdens such as work are to be distributed justly, as are benefits, and this man has refused to do work which could be justly required of him if he were within the system of claims. Insofar as a man refuses to recognise claims of justice made upon him he weakens the claims of justice that he can make on others, just as the claims that can be made within a moral practice grow weaker as the practice becomes more unjust. Justice, as we have seen, is a system of mutual and inter-dependent claims, so refusal to recognise the proper claims made on one weakens the claims that one can make, in the extreme case placing one right outside the system within which claims can be made.

It might be thought that an account of justice which stresses the role of needs leaves a large loophole: cannot injustice be done by exploiting people in such a way as to prevent their forming aims which would give them certain needs just as well as by neglecting the needs that they do have? In a racially divided society, the race in power might decide that it was in their own interests to keep the other race in a state of ignorance and free of education. Because of their ignorance, the subject race would not form certain aims: not knowing anything about refrigerators and coffee vending machines, they could not form the aim of buying or making them. Because they did not have those aims they would not need, in order to achieve their aims, what was needed to achieve those other aims of which they were ignorant. Their standard of living would therefore be lower, and they would form a cheaper source of labour than otherwise, while not feeling that they were oppressed provided that the system of maintaining ignorance was efficient.

The relationship between the powerful and the subject in this case is not co-operative. Whenever I employ somebody to work for me and benefit from his services, I can properly be said to be exploiting him or his labour even if I pay him very generously. To exploit somebody in the pejorative sense, though, is to make use of his services illegitimately, i.e. without due consideration of his needs, work and merit. It is a case of exploitation in the pejorative sense that leads to the objection now being considered, but the objection overlooks the point that, while needs are dependent on aims or goals, they are not required to be dependent on the aims or goals held by those whose needs they are. I pointed out earlier that needs can be discussed in the context of a standard of living and what is necessary to attain that standard of living. Those who exploit somebody else in the required sense prevent him from getting what he needs for a higher standard of living, one that he would enjoy, and one to which his work entitles him. If a man does not want the higher standard of living then he has every right to reject it, but, on the assumption that he would enjoy the higher standard of living, we can quite properly ascribe to him the needs of that standard of living and count them as his needs for the purposes of working out justice. Exploitation overlooks both needs and works.

To say that, on the assumption that somebody would enjoy a higher standard of living, we can ascribe to him the needs of that standard of living even though he has expressed no opinion on the matter, or because of his ignorance, lack of education, or other things of that sort, is in no position to express a proper opinion, sounds paternalistic. In fact, it is paternalistic, but that is no sound objection to it. Refusal to be paternalistic in some cases, such as the obvious one of a father looking after his child, can show injustice through straight-forward failure to perform duties or by showing a lack of concern for the rights and interests of others. Paternalism is not wrong in principle, but it is usually wrong in fact because not many of us are in a position to be justifiably paternalistic towards others. Where we plainly are in such a position, as with infants, the uneducated, and the insane, a paternalistic policy seems unobjectionable, though it needs to be remembered that a good father lets his children make their own mistakes every now and again and tries to bring them up to be independent. That my position allows for paternalism is nothing against it. What has to be shown is that the paternalism is objectionable.

NOTES

1   Perelman, *The Idea of Justice and the Problem of Argument*, (Routledge and Kegan Paul, London, 1963).
2   See, for example, D.H. Monro's review of N. Rescher's book *Distributive Justice* in the *Australasian Journal of Philosophy*, December, 1967.
3   *Op. cit. passim.*
4   *Ibid.* p.53.
5   *Ibid.* p.16.
6   *Ibid.* p.30.

FIVE
An example: murder

Qualifications are needed to make the point precise, but it seems quite plain that it is wrong to kill people. What is not so plain is *why* it is wrong to kill people, especially when one considers that the person killed will not be around to suffer the consequences afterwards. He does not suffer as a consequence of his death, and he need not suffer even while dying. His friends, relatives, and dependents might suffer, but that does not seem to be enough to solve the problem; it is, in the Common Moral Consciousness, just as wrong to kill somebody who has no friends, relatives, or dependents. To think of the wrongness of killing somebody in terms of whether or not it will upset somebody else is to miss the somewhat obscure point completely. The Common Moral Consciousness is quite clear that the reason why it is wrong to kill somebody has something to do with him, not with his mother or maiden aunt, and the Common Moral Consciousness in this context is the concept of murder, not simply common beliefs or conventional morality.

Utilitarianism will not do the job of explaining why it is wrong to kill somebody. The most commonly used of the traditional points against Utilitarianism is that it subjugates the interests of the individual to those of the majority, which could, in the appropriate circumstances, commit a Utilitarian to the view that the execution of an innocent man chosen at random was justified. Negative Utilitarianism, the tenets of which require us to minimize pain rather than to maximize pleasure, has even more radical consequences: as has been pointed out[1], it would require us to kill people painlessly. It does not simply require us to do it painlessly if we must kill people; it requires us to kill people if we *can* do it painlessly. Killing somebody just like that, not in time of war, self-defence, or judicial execution, is ungenerous, unmerciful, cruel, and perhaps arrogant, but none of those words explains what is wrong with it; there is a good deal more to it than that.

Nor is the word 'unjust' one that immediately springs to mind. We could simply intuit the wrongness of killings, but that would not get us far and would leave us with problems in our accounts of moral argument, moral education and theory of knowledge. It is not simply that the consequences of everybody's killing somebody would be unpleasant, either, and it is not that my killing somebody is contrary to the point of an institution required for the performance of the act as breaking a promise uses the institution of promising but goes against its point.

I have asked a few people of my acquaintance what is wrong with killing people, and have received a small range of replies each of which is fairly obviously inadequate. It may be true that killing somebody shows insufficient respect for persons, but there is more to it than that; killing somebody is not, as this answer suggests, morally on a par with spitting in his eye. If I kill somebody then my act is, indeed, unrectifiable, but that does not make it wrong; all that unrectifiability can do is to make something that was wrong anyway into something worse. It is not so obviously true that killing somebody restricts his freedom of action, since he would no longer be around to have any freedom of action, but, even overlooking that problem, killing somebody does more than breaking his leg or locking him up, either of which would involve restricting his freedom of action. Locking somebody up unrectifiably would be more serious, but still the feeling persists that killing him would be wrong in a different way, whether or not it would be worse. Locking somebody up for a long time involves preventing his doing what he wants to do, frustrating him, and perhaps eventually driving him insane; in short, it involves inflicting upon him a good deal of unpleasure. Killing somebody does not thus involve the infliction of unpleasure, or, at least, it need not; the death itself may be painless, and after that the person killed suffers neither pleasure nor unpleasure. Killing somebody may involve denying him equality of rights with me, but it need not; I may be quite prepared to die myself, but it is still wrong for me to kill anybody else. No matter what I plan to do, the lives of others should not depend on my whim. Even if I do not plan to kill myself immediately after killing somebody else, and thus do, in some way, deny my victim equality of rights with me, my killing him is not morally the same as my drinking beer while denying him the right to do so, or cursing around the house and then upbraiding my son for doing the same thing. It may be said that killing is simply more serious, but why? It is not more serious simply in being a denial of equality of rights, and if the point is that the right to live is more important than the right to drink or curse, then nothing is settled: one aspect of the problem from which I began is the problem why the right to live is more important.

So I want to reject all the answers suggested so far, at least in the simplistic forms in which they have been suggested. That there is something in some of what has been said, though, should emerge as we go on.

Moral philosophers, when they do take specific examples, tend to take them from a fairly restricted range and tend to choose them in terms of how well they illustrate a theory. Perhaps they also feel that there is no point in trying to explain something quite as obvious as the wrongness of murder. There are certainly some grounds for saying that explanation should be, not of the obvious, but in terms of it. Unfortunately, very few that I have read have tried to explain the wrongness of killing, and those accounts that have been given are usually notable for their implausibility. In some cases one need only read the account to reject it; argument seems hardly to be necessary. The wrongness of murder is explained by G.E. Moore, for example[2], basically in terms of the fact that murder's becoming a common practice would promote a general feeling of insecurity which would take up time that could be spent to better purpose. Tiddley-winks' becoming a common practice would similarly take up time that could be spent to better purpose. Moore did not leave it at that: it was only occasional murder that he thought he had shown to be wrong; a policy of universal murder is a different thing altogether, and Moore did not think that he could similarly show that to be wrong. He wrote:

. . . the general disutility of murder can only be proved, provided the majority of the human race will certainly persist in existing. In order to prove that murder, if it were so universally adopted as to cause the speedy extermination of the race, would not be good as a means, we should have to disprove the main contention of pessimism — namely that the existence of human life is on the whole an evil. And the view of pessimism, however strongly we may be convinced of its truth or falsehood, is one which never has been either proved or refuted conclusively. That universal murder would not be a good thing at this moment can therefore not be proved.[3]

There is a logical mistake involved in asking whether murder is wrong either as a universal policy or as an occasional pastime; we can intuitively see that murder is wrong because that is what the word 'murder' means. The problem as it arises in the passage I have quoted, can be removed simply by substituting the word 'kill' for the word 'murder'. The problem that arises then is that not all killing is regarded as wrong, and it would be false to say, without my earlier remark about qualifications, that it is quite certain that killing people is wrong. There are various conditions more or less commonly accepted as making it not wrong to kill somebody: I may kill somebody if he threatens to kill me and killing him is my only means of defending myself; I may kill somebody if the leader of my society announces that we are in a state of war with the other person's society; I may kill somebody if he is my slave or a member of another tribe or has passed the age of 65; I may kill somebody if he has committed such crimes as to be declared an outlaw; or I may kill somebody if he is in great and unrelievable pain.

Each of these conditions is more or less widely accepted in one society or another as making killing permissible, so one cannot reasonably say simply that it is quite certain *that* killing people is wrong even if it is not clear *why* killing people is wrong. But certainly some cases of killing people are wrong, and in working out just what makes these cases wrong we ought also to be working out just what conditions make killings permissible. The task which I have set myself, that of explaining what is wrong with killing people, can also be regarded as the task of explicating the concept of murder, and Moore's use of the word 'murder' when he says that a policy of universal murder may be a good thing does not show that his argument necessarily involves a self-contradiction even though his expression of it might.

Nevertheless, the relationship between the concepts of killing and murder explains why we have a feeling, not simply of uneasiness about Moore's argument, but of blank rejection. Moore, it seems, has simply missed the point if he makes his judgment of killing in terms of its utility. The devil may have his due, and if I choose to lead a less pleasant life than I could, or one providing me with fewer goods than I might have, then nobody, one is inclined to say, has the right to stop me. Murder is wrong in itself, and the fact that we have formed such a concept or added such a word to our moral vocabulary suggests that, in the Common Moral Consciousness, those acts of killing which are wrong are regarded as being wrong in themselves, not merely as being disutilitarian. When one man wantonly kills another, not in self-defence or anything like that, but, say, simply because he enjoys killing people, we have no need to wait for the consequences before judging the act to be a murder and therein wrong; as remarked earlier, the reactions of the victims's mother or maiden aunt have nothing to do with the morality of killing.

Were euthanasia legal, a man might make an appointment with his doctor to be killed and thus put out of unbearable pain, but if somebody knowing nothing of this were to break in and shoot him, anticipating the doctor through sheer joy of killing, then that act would be murder and wrong even though it had the same consequences as an act to which no objection would have been raised. We have no need to wait for the consequences before we judge a killing to be murder and thus wrong; the consequences may be good or bad, but either way they are incidental to the morality of the act. A child-murderer's pointing out the high probability of his victim's growing up to be another Hitler has not justified his act though he might have shown that, incidentally, it had done the rest of us a good turn.

If I do not immediately comment on this, I shall no doubt be accused of begging the question. Why are the consequences incidental? To rule them out of consideration by saying that they are incidental, it might be objected, begs the question by building in a moral judgment.

Now, I did not say simply that the consequences are incidental to the act; I said that they were incidental to the *morality* of the act. Whether they are incidental or not to the act depends on how the act is described. If it is described simply as killing, then the consequences may not be incidental to the act; they may be exactly what the killer was aiming at. But the morality of his act does not depend on his having killed, it depends on his having murdered. To put it another way, his act is not wrong *in that it is a killing*, it is wrong *in that it is a murder*. So his act is morally assessed in terms of murder, and so far as the morality of his act is concerned it comes under the description of murder and not simply under the description of killing. At this stage we can say, roughly, that a murder is done if one person intentionally kills another and if none of the conditions defeating a claim of murder are present: the killing was not done in self-defence, nor was it done in time of war, and so on. These conditions do not refer to the consequences, they refer to the intention, knowledge, and mental state of the killer. We can apply the concept of murder without reference to the consequences after death, so the consequences after death are incidental to the act's being a murder.

But what, it might be asked, if people believed that consequences did affect the morality of the killing? Perhaps none of the defeating conditions do refer to consequences, but why should we not introduce a new one that does?

That's the way the world is, that's the way our concepts are; that's where we have to start from. If the world were different (even if only in that people held different beliefs from those they do hold), then our concepts would be different. If *everybody really* believed that when we die we go to heaven — all those grapes, on a hot day there are half a dozen comely angels to fan us, the English never win a test match and there is no tax on beer — if everybody really believed that, then, whether or not their beliefs were true, we probably would not have a concept of murder at all. Our morality and the moral concepts we have would be different. Our concepts are the way they are because the world is the way it is and because people believe, want, and need, what they do believe, want, and need. That is where we have to start from, so that is where I do start from.

None of this is meant to imply that the concept of murder is always easy to apply or that it in no way has any connection with the future tense. That is why there is still equivocation about the child-killer if he can really prove that his victim would turn out to be another Hitler; one really feels uneasy about taking either side in the dispute, which is to say that the concept is difficult to apply in such cases. But what gives rise to the equivocation is not the consequences of the killing, as I have already tried to show. What gives rise to the equivocation is the intention of the agent, which is a different thing. That he did spare us another Hitler is irrelevant; that he intended to do so is not. His intentions, though not the consequences of his act, affect whether of not he has committed a murder; whether his intentions were realized is incidental. If his intention does defeat a claim of murder (as has been argued is the case in assassinations), then it is irrelevant that another Hitler turns up anyway, so that the killer has not spared us that after all.

One thing of importance, then, is the brute fact that excusing and justifying conditions for murder do not refer to the consequences, but there is immediately apparent at least one reason why this might be so: a man from whose act of killing good consequences accidentally flow is a man who kills without any thought of bringing about good consequences, and is therefore as dangerous to have about as any other killer. And if the consequences are not accidental, it is the intentions, and not the consequences themselves, that establish that fact.

So, if an act of killing is wrong, it is wrong in itself and not because of its consequences. For the same reason, the distinction Moore draws between universal murder as a policy and murder as a spare-time hobby is of no moral significance. An individual case of murder is wrong in itself, i.e., wrong in that it is murder. If a policy of universal murder is introduced, the only change made in the situation is that we have a lot more individual cases of murder each of which is wrong in itself. Murders are judged one by one; the number of them has no effect on the wrongness of each. Introducing a policy of universal action can have special effects: introducing a policy of universally doing what we say we will do after uttering the words 'I promise' changes the situation by creating a new institution, that of promising. But introducing a policy of universal murder creates no such new institution and does not relevantly change the situation. Obedience to the rule, 'Always murder', does not even partly constitute a practice; it simply collects a number of individual cases each of which remains what it would have been without the policy: wrong in itself.

There is an argument that might be constructed along lines similar to something that Moore wrote elsewhere, though I have no wish to father the argument onto his moral philosophy. The argument goes like this: I am more certain of the truth of the claim that there is a hand before my face than I could be of any statement used as a premiss in an argument to prove or disprove it.[4] A similar claim about killing might be well calculated to evoke a sympathetic reaction. My initial feeling of uneasiness about such a claim might be explained by a story. Moore's argument took several different examples in his different presentations of it: I am more certain that there is a hand before my face, that I am writing, that I am seated at my desk, that there is a skylight above my head. The argument in the last of these forms, so the story goes, was used by Moore in a lecture in America when, unfortunately, there was no skylight above his head; there was only a patch of light reflected from a window in the wall.

The analogue of Moore's external-world argument was suggested to me by another which I find difficult to pin down with certainty but which I have come across in conversation. It is a sort of paradigm-case argument which could be used in discussion of murder, and I think that there are traces of it in the writings of Anscombe and Geach. If somebody questioned the wrongness of killing people then, according to this argument, we should simply reply in some such terms as these: 'Anybody who doesn't realise that it is wrong to kill people does not understand what morality is; he has a debased conscience and I have no desire to argue with him'. Compare what Anscome says: '. . . if someone really thinks, *in advance*, that it is open to question whether such an action as procuring the judicial execution of the innocent should be quite excluded from consideration — I do not want to argue with him; he shows a corrupt mind'.[5]

It is not clear to me that Anscombe's remark is to be taken as a straightforward example of the paradigm-case argument, as I am setting it up, for killing, since she is, in that paper, frying bigger, or at least more general, fish, but I think that what she says must be at least closely related to the paradigm-case argument. To take over the form of an argument that she uses elsewhere in that paper, judicial execution of the innocent may be a paradigm case of murder; anybody denying that it is murder may be simply pretending that he does not know what the word 'murder' means. To say that, though, does not explain *why* murder is the concept that it is or *what* concept it is. What she says does not finish the matter, and does not make it *philosophically* improper to pretend that it is an open question whether innocent men ought to be judicially executed. So pretending, we might work out why they ought not to be executed and thus learn something about the concept of murder. I should add, lest it seem that I am attacking Anscombe where I am not, that she does not claim that such a pretence is philosophically improper; she claims that regarding the judicial killing of the innocent as a possible course of action is *morally* improper, and that any philosophical theory of morals implying that it should be regarded as a possible course of action is to be dismissed. I have no wish to disagree with her on either count.

Be it Anscombe's argument, one related to it, or even one completely unrelated to it, the paradigm-case argument that I have described is one that could be used to argue about killing people. 'Killing people is a paradigm of wrongness; if you fail to recognize that killing people is wrong then you have a corrupt mind and no understanding of what morality is'. This, no doubt, is significantly different from the analogue of Moore's external world argument, but they share the rejection of the idea that argument is possible, or, anyway, appropriate. This is a dubious, and indeed dangerous, claim about anything to do with morality. For a start, one should be ready to explain to the confused masses why the judicial execution of an innocent scapegoat is not preferable to the death of millions; one should, it is true, also be ready to persuade them of the point, which might be a different matter. Also, the list of conditions which are more or less widely accepted in different societies as defeating a claim of murder needs to be considered; if they are not completely arbitrary (and if murder is a moral concept, then they are not), then they stand in some rational relationship to the concept of murder, and that relationship will help to explain why killing is wrong when it is wrong. So argument about the wrongness of such cases of killing is possible. At least: argument is possible to justify the claim that such cases of killings are wrong. If one is stuck with a borderline case in an argument about a condition purporting to defeat a claim of murder, as one might be in some cases of provocation or of crimes of passion, then argument will clearly be appropriate.

If we take up specifically the external-world analogue, the first point to be made should perhaps be that there is a difference between 'I am certain . . .' and 'It is certain . . .', a point that I tried to make briefly with my reference to Moore's skylight. To say that it is certain that such-and-such is to say something like such-and-such is necessarily true. To say that I am certain that such-and-such, on the other hand, is just to say that such-and-such seems obvious to me, or that I am very deeply convinced of it. But, unfortunately, as we all learned at our first year tutor's knee, our being very deeply convinced of something proves nothing but our own existence. In morals, especially, what one person is firmly convinced of another may firmly disbelieve, and what everybody is firmly convinced of at one time everybody may firmly disbelieve at another. It was once quite firmly believed that slavery was a social system required by justice because slaves were naturally inferior beings, and the belief was shared by even the slaves — or so I'm told. A contrary belief would be fairly widely held today. It was once generally and firmly held that women ought to be subject to their husbands and ought not to have equal rights with men, but things have now changed to the extent that the Women's Liberation Movement has to be taken less as a claim for justice than as a claim to have not only the moon but jam on it as well. There is surely some test for right and wrong in such cases. People changed their minds for reasons; we can, anyway, give some reasons for adverse judgment on the former belief in each of the examples I have cited.

Even if it is obvious that we should not kill people, and even if we are all quite firmly convinced of that, it would not follow that there are no *reasons* for judging killing to be wrong. From finding explanations for the obvious in the physical goings-on around us we gain all sorts of advantages in terms of theories which enable us to predict or explain all sorts of less obvious things.

That does not dispose of all the force of the external-world argument, but what remains does so because that argument can be taken as a version of the paradigm-case argument that I sketched earlier. The point of that argument, in this context, is that it attempts to give grounds for doing away with claims for justification. 'This is red; it's a paradigm case of redness; nothing can or need be done to justify that claim.' How far will the argument go in the moral case?

The idea of a paradigm-case argument being applied to killing has some initial plausibility. One reason for its plausibility is simply that it does seem obvious that killing is wrong but not at all obvious *why* it is wrong. Another reason is that moral education often seems to be carried out in terms of paradigms: we are told that pulling pussy's tail is naughty, or at another level, not to hit little sister, though perhaps the word 'education' ought to appear in inverted commas if such activities are said to be part of moral education. So the argument has some initial plausibility, but in view of the second reason I gave for that it ought to be said that the paradigm-case argument is not a theory of learning or concept-formation though it might rest on one in some way. It is an argument purporting to show that certain claims can be justified or refuted in a certain way. To operate the paradigm-case argument on murder, we should first have to show that we could learn the concept of murder only by ostension. Otherwise, the paradigm-case sort of rejection of a search for reasons would not apply.

Suppose I look at a letter-box and say 'This is red'. If I am idiot enough to say that, somebody else may be idiot enough to ask me to justify my claim. What can I say if he does? 'I see it, and conditions of observation are normal; what more do you want?' This at least looks like a perfectly reasonable rejection of a request for justification. But morality is supposed to be rational; if viciousness does not tie up with reasons for not performing vicious acts, we are stuck with problems about what has been called the action-guiding nature of moral judgments; morality is commonly conceived of as providing and/or assessing reasons for action, whether or not those reasons actually motivate anybody in the situation. If moral concepts are actually taught in terms of paradigms of mere bodily movements and not in terms of reasons, then they do not carry the implications we thought they did. If the claim is not simply that it is obvious *that* killing is wrong, but also that it is obvious *why* killing is wrong, that's fine (though false), but it does not mean that there are no reasons or that we should not give the reasons.

Hobbes thought that murder was a species of injustice, though, as I commented earlier, this is not a word that naturally leaps to mind in connection with killing. He thought that it was unjust partly because he gave a somewhat idiosyncratic account of justice: '. . . when a Covenant is made, then to break it is *Unjust*: And the definition of INJUSTICE is no other than *the not Performance of Covenant*. And whatsoever is not Unjust, is *Just*.'[6] Hobbes's account of justice was straightforwardly in terms of contract; it is unjust to break a contract, just (though perhaps cruel, arrogant, etc.) to do anything which does not involve breaking a contract. In entering social life, each of us has made a contract with each other member of the society not to kill him. There are qualifications of detail, and interesting ones, to be added to this, but that will do for the moment. Each of us has contracted not to kill, so killing is an infringement of contract and therefore unjust. The rest of what I say on the subject of murder will be an attempt to show that Hobbes has the central points of the matter right.

How would killing stand if people actually lived in their natural condition as Hobbes describes it — that is, not simply in a society that lacked a state or any established form of government, but in a world in which the contest always went to the stronger and men killed whenever it suited their interests to do so? In such a situation, with no co-operation between men, we would not have even a society: if, as is often said, morality is man-made in terms of his society, then there will be no morality in the natural condition and men will be free to do what they will. Hobbes has often been interpreted as making just such a claim as this. Specifically with respect to killing (but also, I think, generally), it is an eminently plausible position. If other men killed freely whenever it served their interests to do so, thus placing me in constant fear of death at their hands, it seems that it would not be wrong for me to kill also. Indeed, I might be foolish not to forestall them by killing. Intuitively, it does seem clear that the fact that everybody else killed in this way would be relevant to the morality of my killing. (I shall suggest below that the point is not merely intuitive, at this level anyway.)

If Hobbes is right, as his position has so far been described, the prohibition on killing people is of the same logical sort as the prohibition on promise-breaking; the rule against killing people is a constitutive, not merely descriptive, rule of morality, and there is no obligation to refrain from killing people unless the rule is generally accepted. Actually, for reasons I will explain later, I think that Hobbes saw more than this, whether or not he said more.

His theory as set out so far explains quite a bit about killing. We enter the social contract primarily to protect our lives, and secondarily to make them more enjoyable by making us more secure in our possessions and so on. The points come in that order because we cannot have the enjoyment without having the life. One condition releasing me from the obligation not to kill somebody else, it follows, is that he is trying to kill me; he is then failing to keep his side of the bargain and thus releases me from mine. I promised not to kill him provided that I was given security of my own life, and that condition is not being met. The same holds true of the enemy in time of war. If life begins at forty and ceases to be enjoyable at sixty-five, it might be written into the contract, or be one of the established practices of a society, that out of respect for the aged we shall put them to death when they reach that age. Hobbes's theory, as it stands, gives an explanation of why murder is prohibited, why there are defeating conditions to a claim of murder, why the defeating conditions are what they are, and why they can vary from one society to another (the contracts that were signed differed in details). It also explains why murder, though wrong for reasons of the same logical sort as promise-breaking, is a matter of greater import than is promise-breaking; protection of our lives was the primary reason for our making the contract, and gaining more good things to make life more enjoyable, which promising does, was secondary. These are requirements that any satisfactory answer to the question 'What is wrong with killing people?' would have to meet.

If we do not want to be caught up with the signing of contracts and the requirement that people once did live in their Hobbesian natural condition before the contract was signed, the whole thing can quickly be rewritten in terms of commutative obligation and the established practices in societies as they are. The talk of our reasons for signing the contract can be translated into talk of the benefits we gain from living in a society rather than a Hobbesian natural condition, and talk about primary and secondary reasons can be translated, with the same argument, into talk about the relative importance of the benefits that we gain.

Hobbes' theory as so far described looks fairly neat, but there is an inadequacy in it, and one of which he was aware, whether or not he dealt with it satisfactorily.

THE RIGHT OF NATURE, which Writers commonly call *Jus Naturale*, is the Liberty each man hath, to use his own power, as he will himselfe, for the preservation of his own Nature; that is to say, of his own Life; and consequently, of doing anything, which in his own Judgement, and Reason, he shall conceive to be the aptest means thereunto.[7]

In this passage, Hobbes places limitations on the right of nature. In the natural condition, where others kill whenever it serves their interests to do so, I still cannot do just as I please. He summarizes the point in his second Law of Nature: 'By all means we can, to defend ourselves'[8], and emphasises the restrictions on our freedom in the first: '*Seek Peace, and follow it*'.[9] In a natural condition, where others kill whenever it serves their interests to do so, it is permissible for me to forestall an attempt to kill me by killing whoever would make the attempt; to do so is to kill in self-defence, and in Hobbes' natural condition would be the only way of defending myself short of living as a hermit, which is not always possible. The fact that everybody else kills does affect the morality of killing that I do; it means that the defeating condition of self-defence can be invoked far more often. Even in the natural condition, no matter how others may behave, it is not permissible for me to kill for the sheer joy of it. Even in the natural condition there is a limitation on killing, so the Hobbesian account given so far is inadequate. The reason why killing for sheer pleasure is ruled out, I think, is that the man who does that is not apt to become a social being.

It is not clear that people in a Hobbesian natural condition could have moral concepts; if each man is at war with all others so that there is no community, it is not clear that 'people' in a natural condition would have any concepts above those that the lower animals have. Looking at the natural condition with the concepts that we have, though, we can see that the man who has no desire to kill for pleasure and who is fit to become a social being is a man who has a virtue. In a natural condition, perhaps, no moral distinctions could be drawn, but they can be drawn when we talk *about* the natural condition. In a natural condition the virtue of a man fit to become a social being might not be recognized, but the quality of character that he has is a virtue in that situation because it makes it possible to leave that situation.

Killing is wrong when and because it is murder, which is a species of injustice. If it is asked why we have a concept of murder and why wanton killing is wrong even in a natural condition, the answer is that we could not have a society without a concept of murder. In Hart's terminology[10], killing is contrary to natural law, i.e. a minimum condition for the existence of a society is that there be some prohibition on killing. If people were never tempted to kill each other we should have no need of a concept of murder, but people are so tempted. If people were not so vulnerable there might be less need for restrictions on killing; but we are vulnerable. If people killed promiscuously and we had no security against their doing so, we should have to be prepared to forestall them by killing in our turn (and it would need to be the first turn), so that we should be back in our natural condition.

The minimum condition that must be met by people if they are to co-operate with each other is that they should not kill each other. To have a society is, amongst other things, to have a concept of murder and thus a prohibition on killing. We ought not to kill because, being members of society, we have a concept of murder, and thus recognise an obligation not to kill. To have a concept of murder, or to have the word 'murder' in the language, is to have *general* acceptance of an obligation not to kill; in that respect, it is similar to promising. An individual man might know what 'murder' meant but not recognize the obligation. If he asks 'Why should I not kill people?' he is asking for reasons of self-interest or something of the sort; he is not asking about the morality of killing. That explains why there is a prohibition on killing or why we have a concept of murder. Why the prohibition and the concept take the form they do, and what conditions defeat a claim of murder, are explained by reference to commutative obligation and the established practices of a society.

That we have a society means that we have a concept of murder; without a prohibition on wanton killing, social life would be impossible. This is not to be taken merely as a straightforward empirical claim. Moral concepts can have a point and can have application only amongst people who are imperfect but not wholly bad. That is not merely a causal claim, since it is a remark about the form of the concepts, not about their material elements. It follows that the sort of question being raised could be raised only if people were of a certain very general character, and to work from the premiss that people are so is not simply to make an assumption as to fact; the premiss has a privileged status. People are vulnerable, and people are tempted to kill; without security against their killing, the trust necessary for co-operation and for social life would be impossible. People could not choose differently in this respect in their 'ultimate choice of a moral code', and in this way the morality of murder is different from the morality of promising.

That we have social life, then, means that there is some sort of prohibition on wanton killing, and, unless there are special circumstances, my going against that prohibition would be unjust. By going against it I am arrogating to myself a right which, it follows from the existence of social life, cannot be generally allowed. Unless I have a story of special circumstances marking me off from others, it follows that I have no such right and that I am infringing the rights of whomever I kill; it follows, therefore, that my killing somebody is unjust. The point of co-operation or of social life is the satisfaction of the needs of those in it, and the prohibition placed on killing reflects very basic needs indeed. If I kill, I ignore those basic needs and the claims generated by social life.

The other strand in my account of murder needs to be drawn out, too, lest it be overlooked. This is the strand which covers cases of killings between people who have no co-operative relationship, and will plainly be of importance in dealing with situations such as war. Most of my discussion so far has been about killings within co-operative relationships, and if the account depended entirely on co-operative relationships it would follow that killings outside such relationships were morally neutral. The account that I am giving, though, does not so depend.

What, then, is the morality of killing between members of two separate societies which have not previously come into contact with each other? One could think of this question as arising about the relationship between a colonising power and the natives of a newly-discovered land which it was invading. There is between the two groups no such co-operation as to generate the sorts of claims arising from practices or common social life. What can be said about the morality of the invaders wiping out the natives, or on a smaller scale, of one invader killing one native? There would be no problem about describing such acts as cruel, for exmple, but how does the concept of murder get purchase?

Many things could affect the morality of such a killing, such as whether the native attacked or threatened to attack the invader, but we shall imagine a case of wanton killing. The morality of this action brings us back to the special place that the prohibition on killing has within a society: the man who kills in these circumstances, with no good cause and simply for the fun of it, exhibits a vice. The vice he exhibits is not one like cruelty, either. A man who does all that justice requires of him but is cruel in that he will never under any circumstances do anything more is a man who is unpleasant but can be lived with; a landlord has a right to his rent and can justly insist that it be paid even though in some circumstances it would be cruel for him to do so, but he can fit into social life (though it will not be a very *sociable* life for such a man) as long as he makes only just claims and meets all just claims made on him. A man who kills for the fun of it, on the other hand, is a man not apt for social life at all.

The reason why each society must have some sort of prohibition on wanton killing is also the reason why the norm must be a man who does not kill wantonly and just for the fun of it and why such activities must be discouraged. It is a fact of social life that killing, even *across* social boundaries, must be frowned upon. If this were not the case, then, in the terms of the social contract theorists, no society could ever have been formed. People are people because they are social, and they can be social only because such actions are not the norm and are discouraged. If this point is ignored, then it might seem that my account licenses a man to behave in the manner appropriate to Hobbes' natural condition whenever there is lack of co-operation, whereas that behaviour seems appropriate to Hobbes' natural condition only because it is a condition of actual and open enmity, not merely of lack of co-operation. But my account does not have this consequence. Aptness for social life and an unwillingness to kill, or generally to be violent, unnecessarily and without good cause, are at the forefront of my account.

There might seem to be a counter-example to my thesis in the case of raiding tribes which set no particular significance on the killing of anybody outside the tribe. There are two distinct sorts of cases that might be considered. One is the case of a number of tribes all of whom take this line, and that case poses no problems at all. It is simply a case of the concept of murder being applied in a Hobbesian natural condition, and what was said about that earlier applies here too: where a man of one tribe kills a man of another tribe, any accusation of murder levelled at him can be passed off in terms of self-defence.

The other sort of case is that in which one tribe places no significance on the killing of outsiders and the other tribes do. It seems to me that there are two ways in which the first tribe could argue that their killings of outsiders were not murders, and that in any other case they would have to plead guilty. And to have to plead guilty would be to recognise that they had reason not to act that way and ought not to do so, which is itself to frown upon that sort of behaviour. The first way is that they could argue that their killings of outsiders were not murders because the members of all other tribes were so grossly inferior that a defence of no injustice was always available when one of them was killed. Where no particular act of culpability is required as well, though, this would be at least very close to the claim that the others were not really people and hence that the concept of murder could not apply.

The other way of attempting to pass off accusations of murder would be for them to say that, no matter what the others said, they believed that a Hobbesian natural condition still remained between the tribes. The acceptability of that defence would depend inversely on the strength of the evidence they had to pass over in order to make it.

What all this means is that there must be recognised a prohibition on killing across social boundaries of just the same sort as the prohibitions that must be recognised on killing within a society. The prohibitions are of the same sort, and they must be recognised *for the same reason*: they are necessary if social life, and, therefore, human life, is to be possible. Provided there are people, there must be a general recognition that they ought not to kill wantonly either within or outside their own society. Special circumstances can crop up that would change the morality of particular acts of killing; if a situation similar to the Hobbesian natural condition arose either within a society or between members of different societies, then the morality of killings between those people would be affected. In the absence of such special circumstances, though, it must be recognised that one ought not to kill and that one invades the victim's rights if one does kill. One's act would be of a class general permission for which would make impossible the co-operation that is necessary for social and human life; one thereby invades necessary human rights and one's act constitutes a species of injustice.

It follows from this account of murder that there must be defences against the charge: all and only defences of justice will properly rebut a charge of murder. If murder is a species of injustice, then showing that a killing was not unjust will show, and will be the only way of showing, that it is not a case of murder.

This does not mean that conceptions of murder cannot be wrong or confused. It does not mean that no group of people can ever be mistaken in the conception of murder that they employ; it provides a standard against which they could be judged to be mistaken and a schema with which it will be possible to locate and explain the confusion. But there are only certain ways in which conceptions of murder can be confused, and beyond those limitations the conception would not be one of *murder*.

What has been set out is the structure of the concept of murder: a murder is an unjust killing. Conceptions of murder can therefore differ by differing about what justice requires or allows in the way of killing. These differences could result from differing practices in the two or more societies actually changing what justice requires or allows, in which case we should have two or more quite proper conceptions of murder; or they might reflect mistakes about justice, in which case we should have improper or confused conceptions of murder. Mistakes about justice could themselves be in the conception of justice; a person who thought that justice concerns only needs and not also, say, willingness to take on burdens, or one who accepted an account of justice such as that given by Perelman[11], would have a different conception of murder from somebody who accepted an account of justice such as I have given. Such disagreements would have to be argued out in the appropriate manner by philosophers. Mistakes about justice could, alternatively, reflect mistaken beliefs about the world, such as that slaves really were naturally grossly inferior to the class of slave-owners.

NOTES

1   R.N. Smart, 'Negative Utilitarianism', *Mind*, 1958.
2   *Principia Ethica* (Cambridge paperback, Cambridge, 1959), pp.156–7.
3   *Ibid*. p.156.
4   See G.E. Moore, 'Proof of an External World', in *Philosophical Papers* (Allen and Unwin, London, 1959), pp.146–7.
5   'Modern Moral Philosophy', in *The Is/Ought Question*, ed. W.D. Hudson (Macmillan, London, 1969), p.192.
6   Molesworth (ed.): *The English Works of Thomas Hobbes* (John Bohn, London, 1839–45), Vol.III, pp.130–1.
7   *Ibid*. p.116.
8   *Ibid*. p.117.
9   *loc. cit.*

10   See *The Concept of Law*, (Oxford University Press, Oxford, 1961), pp.189–95.
11   Ch. Perelman, *The Idea of Justice and the Problem of Argument*, (Routledge and Kegan Paul, London, 1963), especially chapter one, which is discussed above.

SIX
Morality, self-interest, and reasons

There is a fairly widely held view that a reason for acting is a fact plus a desire or an attitude. A reason for acting, it seems to be held, must move me to act, and, whatever the state of the world may be, it will be something about the state of me, my attitudes and wants, which will determine whether or not I move. The facts are somehow inert and neutral things towards which we have attitudes or about which we have wants; without the attitude or wants they impel or suggest no course of action rather than any other and provide no reason at all for acting. That there are apples in the orchard is a reason for me to go there if I want apples, to stay away if I cannot bear ever to see another apple again, and no reason for anything at all if I am in a state of complete indifference to apples. The fact by itself provides no reason for acting and, give people as many facts as we may, we can give them no reason for acting unless they have the appropriate wants.

In one way, it is clearly true that what moves me to action is something about the state of me rather than something about the external world. The fact that a lion leaps at me with a threatening roar will not make me budge; if I think it is just Cedric playing another one of his practical jokes and do not believe that I am being attacked by a lion, I shall stay where I am. Even if it is Cedric, though, I shall move as rapidly as I can if I believe it is a lion. The facts do not move me to action; my beliefs about them do. The view being considered goes further than this. The claim is that not even a belief by itself could be a reason. It must be allied with a want or a desire or an attitude.

This sort of claim about the relationship between wants and reasons is clear in A.I. Melden's *Free Action*:

Let us return once more to what we took as our starting point, an agent mindful of what he is doing and acting as he does for a reason. Suppose such an agent driving along the street and suddenly coming to a stop at the curb. His companion asks, 'Why are you stopping here?'. The answer, 'There is a restaurant nearby', may be true, but the statement, while it may inform his companion of a matter of fact, is not offered as a mere statement of fact in the way in which, for example, this might be done if the persons had been concerned to compile a report of the distribution of restaurants in that locality. It is offered rather as a reason for *doing* something, namely, stopping the car. But 'There is a restaurant nearby' would be no reason for stopping the car unless there was something wanted and to be gotten by performing that action — one stops the car in order to go into the restaurant, and one does that in order to get food. And if one wants food, presumably (although not necessarily) one wants it for eating. Normally, the reason given, 'There is a restaurant nearby', will make it clear that one is stopping the car in order to get the food one wants to eat. And in many cases at least, stating a reason for what one is doing is making it clear what it is that is wanted and what it is that one wants to do with the things wanted . . . . In all of these cases, the reason given explains the action of stopping the car by exhibiting it, in the given circumstances, as a case of getting what was wanted.[1]

A similar sort of claim about the relationship between attitudes and reasons is clear in P.H. Nowell-Smith's *Ethics*:

Many philosophers have made the point that every action must have a motive, and that a motive can only be counteracted by another motive; and some have represented choice as simply the victory of the strongest motive or set of concurrent motives. These points have usually been put as if they were psychological laws; but they are really elucidations of the logic of concepts. To say, for example, that every action must have a motive is to state a tautology, since what a man 'did' without a motive would not count as an 'action'. The theory that a motive can only be counteracted by another motive is also a logical rather than a psychological theory. For it is the theory that we use the word 'motive' in such a way that anything which counteracts a motive is also called a motive. In the same way, my lists of pro- and con-attitudes must be so construed that anything which could be offered as a logically good reason for or against doing anything must be included in the lists. By a 'logically good reason' I do not mean a morally good reason; I mean anything which, when offered as an explanation of why someone chose to act as he did, has the force of making further questionings logically odd.

The proposition that any statement which gives a logically complete reason for choice must include a reference to a pro- or a con-attitude is thus a frank tautology.[2]

The theory is adhered to by many people other than Melden and Nowell-Smith, but these two examples will suffice. The claim is that the facts are somehow inert, and that it is our attitudes to, or wants about, the facts that constitute reasons for acting. Whether person P has reason for performing action A depends, in a very strong way, on P and his attitudes and wants.

One important implication of this theory is worthy of note: if a man's reasons for action depend so strongly on his personal wants and attitudes, then a man with strange or nasty wants and attitudes will have reason for doing strange and nasty things, and all the facts with which we present him cannot give him reason to be nice. If he happens to take great joy in torturing children, the rational thing for him to do is to torture children in undetectable circumstances rather than to seek some way of changing his taste. He can be irrational in his choice of means, but he cannot be irrational in his choice of ends. If Nowell-Smith is correct in his claim that 'there are no logical limits to the possible objects of pro-attitudes'[3], and if one can want anything that is logically coherent, then this theory implies that there is no action such that a man cannot have reason for performing it. No matter how distasteful, nasty, or pointless an act may be, if a man has unpleasant or unusual wants he may have reason to perform it.

Facts, on this theory, are inert; they are neutral between actions and provide no reason for doing one thing rather than another. Facts by themselves cannot be assessed as good or bad reasons for doing this or that. Once an agent and his own particular wants are supplied, then facts can be considered as reasons and can give rise to questions about rationality or irrationality. The want supplies the end of the action, and questions of rationality are questions of efficiency in attaining that end. The facts are considered in terms of means, and it is only means that can be assessed as rational or irrational. If, as in Melden's example, I want food, then the fact that there is a restaurant here gives me a reason to stop the car because it provides a means of satisfying that want. If I enjoy nothing more than seeing gore all over the place with no risk to myself, then the fact that I find myself alone with a defenceless child gives me reason to take a baseball bat to his head. The fact that I could never manage to be alone with defenceless children might give me a reason to see a psychiatrist and try to change my tastes. If I have a private income, do not like leaving my house, and can entice defenceless children in there with no trouble, then I have better reason to satisfy my lust by bashing children's heads in than by taking a job as slaughterman with the local butcher. It is, at the very least, fortunate that most of us have more sociable desires.

The essence of rationality on this account, would be the operation of a calculus as in formal logic. The ideas of being unreasonable (rather than irrational) or merely silly are difficult to locate in this schema of rationality. Rationality is achieved when all the moves made are formally valid, and no premiss or conclusion, taken by itself, can be ruled out as wrong. The rational thing for anybody to do depends on what he happens to want; any want is to be considered, and none can be ruled out as irrational. Given the want, we consider the facts to work out the most efficient means. If our calculations are correct, then the resulting action is rational. Reasons are not at all social or inter-personal items, but attach strictly to the wants and attitudes of the agent.

Reasons, then, are really all of the same quite neutral sort. When we distinguish between moral reasons, prudential reasons, and so on, we are really distinguishing between different sorts of wants that plug into the start of the reasoning. Because of the point at which wants plug into reasoning, they cannot be assessed as rational or irrational. To say that we have moral or prudential reasons is to say that we have moral or prudential wants and are aiming, efficiently or inefficiently, at moral or prudential goals. Wants are neither rational nor irrational and there is nothing to choose between them; moral wants are simply some wants amongst others with nothing special about them and moral reasons, consequently, are simply some reasons amongst others. Morality and rationality have no special connection.

The theory does not require that one always explicitly set out the wants or attitudes involved in a reason for acting. Often, when asked for a reason for some action, we do no more than state a fact: 'Why did you turn left there?'; 'Because the hospital is down here'. The theory does allow such answers if they are recognised as being shorthand for a longer story the rest of which is contextually implied. In this case, if the fact I stated is to be taken as an answer to the question, it can be only because I want to go to the hospital, and that want supplies the rest of the story. Similarly, we might simply state a fact and take it that we have given a reason for acting if the relevant want is a very common one, such as a desire to avoid serious accident. If I say to somebody 'One more step and you will be over the cliff' I take it that I have given him a reason not to move forward, but my having given him such a reason presupposes that he has the common want to avoid serious injury. Here again, the theory says, simply setting out the fact provides no reason for acting unless it is taken as shorthand for a longer story including a desire to survive. If the man wants to commit suicide, the fact of which I inform him might provide him with a reason for going forward.

My thesis is that people holding to this theory are wrong. I do not claim that they are idiots; wants and attitudes are important when we consider reasons for acting. But this theory puts wants and attitudes in the wrong place, and it is because the theory makes this mistake that it has such unpleasant consequences. Reasons for acting are related to wants and attitudes, but they are not so related to personal wants and attitudes that they cannot lead us to curb our wants or to worry about the development of a callous attitude towards children. Some of what Kant said about the relationship between wants and reasons for acting is incomprehensible and some of it is no better than odd, but he was right, I think, in claiming that action merely from wants is animal and that there must be some distinction between wants and reasons so that wants can drive us one way and reasons another, the tension that Kant thought gave rise to the concept of obligation.

Our wants and attitudes are reflected in the very way we see the world and categorise the things in it. The world is not broken up into natural classes, but it is natural that we, with the interests, needs, wants, and desires that we have, should break it up in various ways. We learn to discriminate between things and to classify in many different ways, and the development of these discriminatory and classificatory abilities is what we call the formation of concepts. If we need food, it is natural that we should distinguish food from other things, particularly from poisons. If extremes of heat or cold cause us suffering or even death, it is natural that we should distinguish temperatures and make allied distinctions such as those between the seasons. These distinctions must be drawn if we are to survive, or to live comfortably. Walking naked in the snow can cause a nasty cold, and eating whatever happens to come to hand without considering whether it is nut cutlets, lighter fluid, or ground glass can have even more dire effects, so it is part of human life that such distinctions are drawn.

We must draw such distinctions in order to meet the needs that people in fact have, so concepts such as food are formed in response to those needs. It is needs that give point to the concept and determine the classification. There is no particular drop of one degree Celsius that gives us the change from mild to cold temperatures, because human response to temperatures simply is not like that. The need to which that concept answers does not require, or even allow, so precise a distinction, and it is the need that gives point to the concept and in response to which we discriminate in making the classification. The same need plays a part in the formation of other concepts such as the concepts of house and clothing. One of the functions of houses and clothing is to help us to deal with the weather and our vulnerability to it.

More subtle distinctions can be made. Partly because we have taste as well as a need for food, such concepts as staleness are formed. Because we respond in a variety of ways to a variety of dietary deficiencies we form other concepts such as green vegetable (are red cabbages green vegetables, and why?), protein, and so on. We could even form a concept in this way and then go on to discover what the particular susbstance is that the concept refers to, in the same way as happened with genes. We have big needs to which such concepts as food respond, but we have lots of other little needs, wants, and interests to which other concepts respond.

The distinctions that we draw might not each be a response to only one need or interest. Our need for protection from extremes of weather might lead us to distinguish different seasons in the year, but our need for food, too, given the way the world works and the way plants grow, might also lead us to distinguish seasons. Because of the way the world works, the two needs are met by the same distinction.

When we have a classification such as this, with more than

one point, difficult cases can arise if something new about the world is discovered or if something is brought to light which can be classified in two different ways, with two quite different points. The biologist and the moralist have different concerns in their concept of person, so they can differ quite violently about whether a foetus is a human being. If the case is sufficiently different from the range in the context of which the concept was formed, as brain-transplant cases are outside the range for personal identity, then it might be not only difficult, but impossible. After the brain-transplant there might be no answer to the question whether we have John Smith on the left and Bill Brown on the right, because it is at least possible that our concept of person simply does not cover that case. Instead of arguing about who is which person, we might have to take the argument to a more basic level in terms of the point of the classification, arguing about who is John Smith in terms of why it matters who is who, asking such questions as 'Which one should we employ as accountant and which one should we play as goalkeeper?'. If the question is 'Which one inherits from John Smith, Snr., there might be no answer, or if there is an answer it might be 'Share it half and half'.

Difficult cases, though conceptually less puzzling, can arise when there is only one need to which the concept answers. Something which sustains life but makes one feel very ill is marginally food. That sort of case is less puzzling because the answer comes out in terms of the point of the concept, whereas the problem about John Smith is that two different points of the concept seem to come into conflict.

Our concepts might not answer to only one or two needs. The ways in which we distinguish animals might be responses to various needs: our need for food, our need or desire not to be wounded, our need for clothing to protect us from the cold, and so on. We classify things because we need to. There is a point to our doing so, and it is that point that determines whether or not our classification is correct, or what comes into the class and what does not.

Our lives require that we deal with people as well as with the rest of the world around us. What we can do in our daily lives depends on what other people do, what they will let us do, what they will help us do, and what they will prevent our doing. We often need to co-operate with people, and we often need to know what they will do. We therefore need to distinguish between statements that somebody is likely to do something, statements of intention, promises, and so on. Once we have drawn these distinctions, with the point there is to drawing them, it is plain why different responses are appropriate if somebody does not do what he said he was likely to do, or what he said he intended to do, or what he promised to do. Because we live with people and need to co-operate with them, we distinguish virtues from vices. Because we want to be amused but not upset, we distinguish what is funny from what is in bad taste.

That there is something or other five miles NNE of Ayers Rock is not sufficiently important for a concept of something or other five miles NNE of Ayers Rock to have been formed; concepts are formed because they are important in one way or another, and it is their importance that makes them operable. An attempt to reply to this by forming the concept *clob*, meaning 'something five miles NNE of Ayers Rock', and thereby produce a concept with no importance, is doomed to failure. Consider the unanswerable questions that immediately arise: what counts as a something or other? A pile of sand? A historical site? A vacuum? A camel train on the move? Does the something or other remain a clob when it changes location? Or changes shape? How precisely are the five miles and the NNE measured? How big is a clob? If there is a large rock there, is the whole rock a clob or only the centre? The part at ground level? And so on. There is no obvious limit to the questions that can be asked to which the concept *clob* gives no answer. The point is not simply that difficult cases arise or that answers are not always possible in terms of the concept *clob*; as we have seen, that can happen even with perfectly respectable concepts such as *person*. The puzzlement is different, because the concept *clob* suggests no way in which we might try to sort out an answer or carry the argument further. Any attempt to deal with that problem would involve giving a point to the concept or explaining why it mattered whether or not something was a clob. Each of the questions I have listed might be answered *ad hoc* with no suggestion of why the answer should be the one given, and hence no point given to the concept, but that does not deal with the apparently open-ended list of questions that I have not set out.

Some of our concepts are formed directly in terms of our needs, wants, desires, and so on for action. The, or a, need met by some of our concepts is to make plain why some line of action is appropriate; that is the point of the concept. Such concepts are not uncommon. It is not, *pace* Nowell-Smith[4], simply a matter of fact that people by and large do not want to be bored. That is the point of the concept, and if we find somebody seeking boredom (not simply seeking a quiet life) then we have to look for a special story or the situation is incomprehensible. His response, 'Because it is boring', does not give an answer to the question 'Why are you doing that?'. If he seriously thought it did, just like that, then that would be a ground for regarding him as mad. He would need a special story such as that, while he did not like being bored, he did want to do penance and that involved subjecting himself to things he did not like. That is to say, he would need a special story bringing the boredom under a different concept. The fact that a book is boring is a reason not to read it, albeit a reason which might be outweighed if, say, the book also contained information that one needed.

We have already discussed one action-guiding concept at some length: the concept of murder. That a killing would be murder is a reason for me not to perform it whether or not I want to and whether or not I actually refrain. If I should go ahead and commit murder, then my action is contrary to reason and properly describable as unreasonable. Social life is possible only if we have some prohibition on wanton killings and thus presupposes a classification of prohibited killings or a concept of murder. Were the prohibition not accepted and generally obeyed, we should have no social life. To put it another way, one presupposition of social life is that the fact that a killing would be murder is a reason for not carrying it out. A murder is a wrongful killing, one that ought not to be performed, and, as we have seen, the classification is not made in terms of the wants, needs, and interests of the prospective murderer, so the reason is not dependent on his wants, needs, and interests.

As was pointed out in the earlier discussion of murder, the reason for refraining from a killing is simply that it is murder. The reason is not that social life will collapse in the face of an isolated murder and that the murderer will suffer in the absence of any social life. Social life plainly survives a great number of isolated murders. The possibility of social life is not the reason for refraining from killing; its role is to explain why we have a concept of murder, why the prohibition is necessary, and why the fact that a killing would be a murder is a reason for not performing it. The possibility of social life is not itself one of the reasons, but rather operates behind the reasons by informing the concepts. That a killing would be murder is a reason for not performing it. That that is a reason is forced on us by the facts of human life, not by the wants, needs, and interests of some particular potential murderer.

This is the quickest possible sketch of an account of reasons that I shall build up in this section. Social life may well depend on certain facts about human nature, and those facts may be necessary to explain how reason can be practical, but neither social life nor reasoning depends on the psychology of any particular person. If human life does presuppose the use of certain moral concepts and the acceptance as reasons for acting of facts involving them, then moral reasons are not simply some reasons amongst others, and people with some sorts of wants have reason to change them rather than to try to satisfy them.

There is a long-standing belief amongst philosophers that reasons for acting must attach to self-interest. The main opposition has been from a view of the sort that we have been discussing, according to which reasons are simply beliefs from which inferences are drawn and what we get out of them depends on what we add to them. Reason considered in this light is ineluctably theoretical and can never move anybody to action. The motive force will be something else, a desire or a want or something of the sort, and reference to the interests or desires of another may move one, or give one a reason for acting in the only sense in which we can understand these words within this theory, if one wants either to benefit or to harm the other. On the other account of what constitutes a reason for acting, too, one can have reasons of direct self-interest for performing an act which incidentally benefits others, but that the act will benefit others can itself be a reason for one to perform it provided that there is more to the story: the benefit that one gives to others will eventually return to one. The point made is simply that it can be in one's interests to co-operate with others.

It is far from clear that philosophers have always distinguished these two views of reasons for acting, and it might be best to regard them as idealised straw men. A philosopher who emphasizes the notion of self-interest in reasons for acting may do so because he is concerned that his arguments should hold for the hard-headed man who will say that facts about other people's interests do not provide reasons for him. That seems to have been Mrs Foot's concern at one time. It might well be felt that nice people who do care about others anyway are no bother and that the arguments should be directed only to the nasty man who cares about nobody but himself. Anybody, it is assumed, will be persuaded by references to his own interests. This is odd, though. Plainly, such reasoning need not persuade people, and in some cases some people might be grossly offended at the idea that showing an action to be in their interests was in any way to give them any reason at all for acting: 'It is in my interest to betray my best friend. You think *that* is a reason for me to do it? You think I should even *consider* that sort of thing when he is trusting me? What do you take me for?'. To say that such a person *has* been given a reason for acting but that the reason in terms of his own interests has been over-ridden by others will not do except as a declation of war; all the argument is yet to come, because it is just that claim that my hypothetical offended agent is denying. He denies that the reference to his own interests gives him any reason at all; in such a context, he is saying, that sort of consideration is simply irrelevant. In making that claim he is not making an obvious mistake; argument will be needed to show that he is wrong.

The philosopher who wants to connect reasons for acting with self-interest can respond to such a man in either of two ways. He can say that such a man is all very well and there should be more like him, but that it is the 'hard-headed' man who poses the problem and that it is to him that the arguments are directed. Alternatively, he can simply say that such a man is a dupe. My interest is in the philosopher who takes the second of these two lines.

The strength of the first account of reasons for acting can be seen most clearly in moral philosophy. Part of the problem is that moral philosophers have called upon the notion of reason for acting without analysing it, and moral philosophy without philosophical psychology is walking on one leg. Recent discussions of the question 'Why should I be moral?' have emphasised the role of prudence on the assumption that any answer not showing morality to be in the agent's interests is unsatisfactory. The usual sort of reply to this claim has been that morality, when reduced to prudence, ceases to be morality at all; virtue is its own reward, it does not produce any other. The reply is, I think, correct, but it misses the point and allows the problem to continue nagging. To say that morality is *sui generis* and cannot be reduced to prudence does not reach the forces which have led so many moral philosophers to attempt to reduce morality to prudence or to answer the question 'Why should I be moral?' in terms of prudence.

The giving of reasons must come to an end somewhere, but it is to be hoped that it does not come to an end just anywhere. Morality is a matter of some significance, and it would lose much of that significance if it proved to be merely arbitrary. To say that morality requires the acceptance of facts about the good of others as reasons for acting, and that attempts to reduce it to prudence overlook this essential point, itself overlooks the problem of explaining why morality is not arbitrary. Why should one bother oneself about the welfare of others? Suppose one doesn't care about others? It might be replied that morality is *sui generis*, that one cannot give non-moral reasons for being moral, and that, consequently, one simply either is moral or is not, and that is all there is to it. But if the acceptance as reasons for acting of facts about the good of others is something we simply either do or don't do, then it is no different from and no better than the acceptance as the most important sort of reason for acting of facts about the day of the week, the colour of flowers, or the welfare of trees. The giving of precedence to people over trees is arbitrary. If the claim that morality is *sui generis* and cannot be reduced to prudence has this consequence, then it leaves morality in no better a position than does the theory it rejects. Morality may be concerned with the good of others and not simply with one's own good, but it is also important and not simply a matter of making any arbitrary choice.

People need not be sociable, but they necessarily are social beings; a man can recognise himself only in terms of a community, because he can recognise himself only in terms of concepts which he gains from communal life even if he later secedes from the community and becomes a hermit. The relationship between people and communities is significant in two different sorts of ways, both tending to show that it is no accident that people live in communities.

In a purely matter of fact way, human life is dependent on the existence of communities of one sort or another. Some creatures are capable of caring for themselves from the moment of birth. Many snakes and sharks are of this sort, but human beings and many birds are not. A human baby abandoned at birth will die; it needs others to feed it and to protect it against the elements and other dangers. This being so, the fact that there are people makes it inevitable that there should be communities of people even if they are shifting communities and do not last for very long. Any newborn baby close at hand is a more easily reached source of meat than is a sitting bird on the other side of the paddock. If people did have a natural predisposition to look after themselves alone then babies would not survive and the human race would disappear, so the fact that the human race continues gives some reason to believe that a fair number of people, for one reason or another, are not so predisposed. Whether it be somehow innate, a matter of upbringing, or something else, it is no accident that people by and large turn out this way. It must be false that people are entirely selfish and moved only by their own narrow interest. A purely selfish man who produced selfish children in the Hobbesian natural condition for any reason other than to provide food would be no better than a fool, since he would simply be multiplying his enemies.

The weaker claim that most men, while not entirely selfish, will send others to the wall rather than go themselves, when it comes down to that, might well be true, but it is much weaker than the claim that people simply do not care whether somebody else goes to the wall or not or that they positively enjoy seeing it happen. Again, the claim that distant disasters do not affect us, or that a man's natural affections extend only over a limited sphere, is a much weaker claim which is no doubt true.

Consider Hume's point:

> . . . justice takes its rise from human conventions; and . . . these are intended as a remedy to some inconveniences, which proceed from the concurrence of certain *qualities* of the human mind with the *situation* of external objects. The qualities of the mind are *selfishness* and *limited generosity*: And the situation of external objects is their *easy change*, join'd to their scarcity in comparison of the wants and desires of men.[5]

I have no desire to go all the way with Hume, but, as is usually the case, there is much to what he says in this passage. Were there no competition for the goods of life, or were men not inclined to try to satisfy their own interests, then we should have no need for moral concepts. Any concepts formed would lack the point of moral concepts and would not, therefore, be moral concepts. But another condition of the possibility of forming such concepts is that men have limited generosity, or that they not be totally selfish. Either unlimited generosity or no generosity at all would rule out the possibility of moral concepts.

If no man ever pressed his claims, but willingly and eagerly gave up everything possible for the good of another, there would be no question of adjudicating claims and no point to a concept of justice. Justice deals with claims, and unlimitedly generous men would have no use for the concept of a claim. If men were unlimitedly generous so that they never felt the slightest temptation to keep something for themselves if another could use or enjoy it, then concepts such as kindness and cruelty would have no point. It is the function of such concepts to guide our behaviour in certain ways, but in the imagined situation our behaviour could not be so guided and the function would not be there to be served. There would be no point or function to inform moral concepts such as we have seen to be necessary for any concept. Problems might arise as such men quickly passed on to others what had generously been given to them, so that nothing was ever actually used. They might even starve.

Again, if men were totally self-interested, concepts such as justice, kindness, and generosity could serve no guiding function and therefore would lack the point they must have. This time it would not be that such concepts were merely redundant pointers to a trail along which we rushed willy-nilly, but just the opposite: if people were totally self-interested, then the concepts could not guide us to that trail no matter what.

This point would not hold were moral concepts merely a species of self-interest concepts, but plainly they are not. Moral concepts do deal with the interests of each person, though not with the interests of any particular person. Those interests inform the concepts, but it is important that we put them in their correct place. I am indeed better off if everybody is just than if nobody is, but I do not work out what is just by calculating what is most in my interests, or even by calculating what is most in my long-term interests allowing for everybody else's reaction to my behaviour. If I have been dishonest, then I have been dishonest even if I have not been found out or even suspected and have escaped with unsullied reputation. In such a case, considerations of honesty and considerations of self-interest would lead me in two quite different directions. One undiscovered act of dishonesty will not harm my interests by causing the collapse of the system of relations on which I depend, and if there were enough dishonesty around to cause such a collapse then I should be a confused fool rather than a moral man if I refused to join in. Morality may serve our interests, but it is not marked out by calculating self-interest, and moral concepts are not shorthand self-interest concepts.

We should expect communal life to be important to people, and we should expect many people to be inclined towards it and to show some degree of sympathy with their fellows. The benefits that follow from having any sort of communal life rather than none at all are immense, as Hobbes showed. One person by himself can do very little in the way of defence against the depradations of villains; even the strongest are vulnerable when they sleep. All the benefits that come from full-time research or from division of labour depend on co-operation. But more than this: co-operation is not simply the course to be chosen by rational but non-social people living their discrete lives with no co-operation. Co-operation is the course for people. Those people could not have been non-social beings leading discrete lives with no co-operation. Without social life and the co-operation it involves, we could not recognise ourselves and could not be human.

Social life involves co-operation and therefore justice. The co-operation required is not simply that involved in planting the corn, watering it, weeding it, and harvesting it, because a man might do all those things by himself. The resolving of disputes or potential disputes is itself a co-operative enterprise distributing benefits and burdens, determining that one is to have his way and another is not. There are clashes of interests which people care about and which, other things being equal, they would press, and that is a presupposition of there being the point to having moral concepts, which gives them form: that people come into at least potential conflict, though with good will they may avoid actual conflict. Good will may ensure that they will find a way to resolve or avoid conflicts, but is not itself a way of doing that or of doing anything else. It is because of this potential conflict that limitation and guidance of behaviour are necessary if we are to retain the harmony that is required for co-operation.

This does not mean that there must be coercion. The limitation and guidance of behaviour in terms of moral concepts may be self-imposed, somebody deciding that he will not press his interests in a given case because to do so would be unfair, unkind, or something of the sort. Even though the limitations may be self-imposed, they along with the guidelines must be commonly accepted by the people concerned if clashes are to be avoided, so the harmony involves co-operation in the settling of disputes. The workability of even self-imposed limitations depends on this co-operative framework. Reciprocity is at the core of the whole thing: what is required, self-imposed or not, is mutual limitation. My limiting myself is improper and silly if you do not limit yourself. We must co-operate with respect to the set of limitations constituting the practice by means of which we resolve disputes.

One implication of this should be emphasized immediately, even before we proceed with the rest of the argument. If we imagine somebody who refuses to co-operate, we usually imagine a man who lives in his own apartment, refuses to take part in making a roster to care for the communal garden, will not join a car pool, and so on. We imagine a man who tries to be self-sufficient, keeping his own things to himself and not making use of others' things. Within the practical possibilities, that is as much as we could imagine. But if we want to imagine a world in which people do not co-operate at all, we need to go further. We cannot imagine a world in which people simply make do with their own things, because, in the absence of co-operation in the form of conventions or decision-procedures determining which is whose, nobody has his own things. We cannot simply imagine a world in which people carefully stay within the sphere of their own rights and make no special claims on others, because, by removing co-operation, we have placed people in an extreme Hobbesian natural condition where there is no sphere of one's own rights. By removing co-operation from the world entirely, we take away all decision-procedures at all levels. Co-operation is so much an assumed part of our lives that it is often difficult to see how much we must take away in removing it. Life without co-operation is a war of each against all because there is no other way of resolving disputes or settling clashes. To introduce a peaceful way which participants in a dispute will accept is to introduce co-operation.

The methods by which we resolve disputes may be of various sorts. Between men of good will they may usually consist simply of discussion and a joint working out, in terms of shared guiding concepts, of the right thing to do. Even men of good will, though, will sometimes disagree about who actually did what in which circumstances, and even if they agree about all of those things, they could still honestly disagree about whether Dudley and Stephens were guilty of murder. In such cases there must be reference to a different sort of decision-procedure in an attempt to resolve the disputes fairly.

It is not that we proceed from our own imperfect notions of justice to a perfect notion in order to settle the dispute; we simply have recourse to a different way of settling the dispute, and, as our men of good will were trying to be just in the first instance, so they try to be just in the second. They might simply submit the case to a third person agreed by both, toss a coin (not as silly as it sounds, given that the justice of the original situation was sufficiently complicated for good-willed men to be unable to resolve a dispute about it), go to court, hold a referendum amongst all those affected, or whatever. Here, at the level of this second-order set of limitations, arises the state.

Given the qualifications set out earlier, our co-operation with respect to such a decision-procedure could impose on each of us in any given case an obligation to accept the result arrived at even if it was at variance with his own original opinions on the matter. As a result of such a decision-procedure's operation, it may become clear to us that, though we have not changed our minds about the dispute to be resolved, it would now be unjust for us to do what we formerly believed justice required of us. The new circumstances of our co-operation with respect to the decision-procedure changes the justice of the situation just as other practices change the justice of other situations. My having to submit to the views of others on the justice of the situation may not please me, but it is not unfair. The dispute had to be resolved, and those concerned disagreed about what was just, so somebody had to submit. That the strongest should always have his way does not guarantee justice; it is certainly no better in that respect than is tossing a coin, and will not generate any obligations as will co-operating with respect to tossing a coin to distribute the burdens and benefits of submitting or having one's way.

Whether disputes be resolved by discussion in terms of shared guiding concepts or by reference to a second-order decision-procedure, reciprocity is central to the whole concern. Unilateral self-imposed limitation cannot achieve the same thing. I may restrict myself to what I regard as just, and others may restrict themselves to what they regard as just, but this gives us no way of dealing with situations in which we differ about what is just or cannot agree on what the facts are. And for me to restrict myself when others will not recognise limitations is, as I have already argued, foolish rather than virtuous. Mutual limitations are required.

Coercion by itself cannot do the job. A dispute between two people is settled only when it is settled for both of them. What is required for settlement of a dispute is mutual acceptance of the result, and that can be achieved only by coercion or co-operation. Either we agree on some method for resolving the dispute, such as tossing a coin or appealing to an arbiter, thus co-operating in settling it, or one of us forces his will on the other. Many disputes, of course, are settled by coercion, but that cannot be the only method; coercion can be effective only against a background of other ways of resolving disputes. If coercion were the only method of resolving disputes, then we should live in a Hobbesian state of nature. Our situation would be a war of each against all, with no mine or thine beyond what one could grab and hold. The conventions specifying property and rights, or the specific forms that rights would take, would be absent because they are co-operative in their mutual recognition of limitations. It is not merely that one would have no right to one's food or house; one would have no right against attack from others, either. Life would indeed be solitary, poor, nasty, brutish, and short.

What is described here is relations between people, not relations between family groups; one should not imagine that one's offspring would have any special status. They would simply be enemies, or potential enemies in a state of great weakness of which one would be foolish not to take advantage. Life would be very short indeed. Every other person would benefit me only accidentally, if at all, and would be prepared to harm me deliberately. He would pose a threat in that he would attack me if our interests clashed or if he thought that they did. Each person would stand to each other person in this relation, and no person would have a right against attack by others. Simply as a matter of self-defence, one would need to miss no opportunity to take advantage of weakness in another and remove the threat; he would pose a threat all the time, without waiting for a clash about who would have some particular wild strawberry. This would be no social life and a very short-lived human race that died out after one brief generation. Since the human race survives, it follows that coercion cannot be the only way of resolving disputes and plays its role only against a backdrop of other decision-procedures. That is, and must be, the nature of the world in which we are born and in which we grow up.

If a man of good will intruded into this Hobbesian state of nature, caring about others, giving up his own interests in favour of theirs, trying to pacify disputants, and so on, then he would be lucky to last five minutes. He will survive only in a society with other good-willed men; in the unco-operative Hobbesian natural condition he is no more than an easy mark. If we introduced enough men of good will into that condition, then the war of each against all would cease; the willingness to simply do battle for whatever one wanted would be much less. But this would not give us an unco-operative Hobbesian natural condition in which there was no war of each against all and disputes were not settled by coercion; it would give us a group of people who, because they are good willed, abandon coercion as a method of resolving disputes and replace it by co-operation, agreeing on mutual limitations for the peaceful settlement of clashes. They would have left the Hobbesian state of nature and entered one much more Lockean because co-operative. It is no accident that people in the Hobbesian natural condition are depicted as self-interested.

The claim that there are, at least potentially, disputes and that they can usually be resolved is plainly true, but it is not intended to simply have the status of an obvious empirical truth. If it is disputes or clashes of interest that give point or form to moral concepts, it follows that there are disputes or clashes of interest whenever questions of or about morality can be raised. Since I am raising a question about moral reasons, it follows that I can properly start from the premiss that there are clashes or disputes. This is something which, in the context, cannot be doubted, and I cannot be expected to worry now about what would be true if there were none.

Co-operation, then, and a willingness to co-operate, are presupposed by social life. If our humanity, and the language and reasoning powers that go with it, depend on social life, then those things, too, depend on co-operation and a willingness to co-operate.

The requirement made of human nature here is that one be prepared to co-operate with other people, and the requirement takes its grip at a very basic stage. It plays its part in making reasoning possible; it comes before acting on reasons, whether they be good or bad reasons, and so before we can draw significant distinctions between people. In the case of co-operation, then, a point applies similar to the one that explained the wrongness of murder committed across social boundaries: the man who is unwilling to co-operate shows himself not apt to be a social being and therein displays a vice. At this stage he cannot reason and therefore cannot have reasons for refusing to co-operate with any particular person; the reasons come in later. So the assumption must be that nobody who can co-operate will be excluded from the co-operation, and then the point of the co-operation will provide the reasons for excluding anybody from it. It might be that somebody is simply unable to do the sort of work involved in a particular co-operative enterprise; that would be a reason for excluding him. Or his record might show that he is likely to make his claim on the benefits but skip his share of the work, which, again, takes away from the effectiveness of the co-operation. Or it might be, less particularly, that simply having too many people in the enterprise could make it ineffective; that might be so if the point of the enterprise was to make a profit sufficient to support all of its members. But in each case it is the point of the enterprise that determines the reasons for excluding people from co-operation. Excluding people on other grounds, such as that they are Negroes, Jews, women, or men applying for a place in an enterprise staffed mainly by men, shows the vice of injustice in a lack of aptness for social life. On the other hand, there is no injustice in a man's insisting that his housekeeper be Scottish if the point of the enterprise is to keep him content, or in the exclusion of unilingual Englishmen from the East Perth Italian Social Club.

Reasons are not simply there any more than anything else is simply there. They, too, have to be picked out by people, and there is a principle of classification determining what counts as a reason and what does not. The concept of reason, like all other concepts, has a point, and it is in terms of that point that the concept must be understood. To know what reasons are, we need to have some idea of what they are for.

Reasons are to justify and explain. That is the point of the concept of reason, and it is in terms of these functions of reasons that we can understand what is involved in something's being a reason. We worry about reasons because we want to know why somebody did what he did and whether it should have been done, and those considerations are important because they affect our reactions and our plans about what we, in turn, shall do. It matters why people do what they do, and it matters whether they did what they did for the right reasons; it matters because it affects what other people can and should do. That is why we need the classification *reasons* and it is how that concept is informed: it is the principle of classification or discrimination determining what counts as a reason and what does not.

The reasons why somebody did what he did matter because they matter to people other than him alone. Explaining and justifying are inter-personal activities. I can explain or justify my actions to myself only in a way derivative from the inter-personal activity, standing back and considering the me who performed that action yesterday or who is contemplating action now as a separate person from the one seeking the explanation or justification. If I am the only one that I have to satisfy, then I can do whatever I want to do; justification is pointless in isolation. Justification comes into the picture when I go beyond the question of what I want and measure my proposed action against some inter-personal standard, one that could also, at least in principle, be used by other people or to judge the actions of other people, even if, in the particular case, I am the only person in a position to know whether my action meets that standard. In working out what to do, or deciding whether my proposed action would be proper, I must be careful to go over the relevant considerations impartially, and that involves treating myself, at least hypothetically, as one amongst others and as having no special place amongst them. If I am really trying to reason out what to do, then I cannot make special allowances for me simply because I am me. Failing in such a way to be impartial is not reasoning, but is simply acting on inclination. (I might, of course, even as a result of reasoning, decide to act on inclination because, say, it does all of us a bit of good to let our hair down every now and again.) The same inter-personality is reflected in the relation between reasons and consistency. It is an important part of the logic of reasons that whatever is a reason for one person is a reason for anybody similar who finds himself similarly placed. One might, of course, have reason to do something that nobody else would ever have reason to do, either because everybody else was different in the relevant respect or because the circumstances were unique, but, again, the logic of reasons requires that one be able to make at least that hypothetical extension to other people. The notion of reason makes sense only in this context of inter-personality.

Reasoning is, logically, an inter-personal activity. It makes sense only in a context of inter-personal relations, of people reacting to each other in some sort of communal life. It presupposes a context of people sharing concepts, and sharing especially those action-guiding concepts constituting the standards invoked in justification. In that it involves this context of a communal life with people interacting, it involves, as we saw earlier, co-operation and a recognition of mutual limitations. Reasoning is an inter-personal or social notion that presupposes whatever is presupposed by social life or this sort of human interaction.

What this argument shows is that reasoning must be inter-personal in principle. It does not show that one must always reason out loud and to others, or that one can never reason silently or when alone. Departure from company does not take away one's ability to reason. But the argument does show that the conditions for the use of reasoning must be met even when it is not actually being used inter-personally. I can reason when I am on my own, but only in ways in which I could reason if others were around. Not just *any* step from one proposition to another is reasoning even when I am in solitary confinement, and what counts as a proper step from one proposition to another, or from propositions to an action, is determined by the inter-personal background against which reasoning takes place.

The connection between co-operation and justice needs little drawing out now since it was discussed at some length earlier. The two are analytically connected, and those who show a willingness to co-operate show, in that, a sense of justice. What one needs to bear in mind is that people have, from time to time, had odd ideas about what is just. They have believed that slaves were sub-human and that kings were representatives of God, believing, therefore, that the relevant form of discrimination in each case was quite just. Exploitation, when it is recognised by the participants as such and carried on with no respect for a sense of justice, will not serve the function of co-operation for the same reason that coercion and unilateral self-imposed limitations are inadequate.

Social life is necessarily co-operative in its resolution of potential disputes, and because it is co-operative it presupposes people with a sense of justice. Reasoning presupposes a context of social or inter-personal activity and it, too, therefore, presupposes people with a sense of justice, so that moral reasons seem to be not merely some reasons amongst others, with no special place, just as well ignored as paid attention. That there is an activity of reasoning presupposes a special place in that activity for reasons of justice. If reasoning is a distinguishing mark of human beings, then human life presupposes the operation of a sense of justice.

There might be, or there might have been, a linguistic community with no word properly translatable by the English word 'justice', and that community might manage to survive because it has a set of taboos appropriate to the purpose. In some cases, religious precepts might provide the controls necessary to allow the communal life to continue. Many accounts of what are often called primitive societies suggest that the controlling of a society by taboo or religious precept rather than by a well-articulated concept of justice is fairly common. If this is possible, let alone actual, it might seem to go against the claim for which I have been arguing.

Despite its appearance, the possibility of a community with no word translatable as 'justice' does not go against my argument. I have made no claims about sounds that people must utter or words that they must use. There might be disagreement about what it is for somebody to have a concept, and that disagreement might or might not be reducible to a difference in stipulative definitions, but I have, throughout my discussion of the sense of justice, emphasized the function of various attitudes and ways of discriminating in social life. The communities described in setting up this objection, while they may lack a word translatable as 'justice', quite plainly do not lack ways of discriminating between the relevant sorts of actions. I suggested earlier that concepts, including the concept of justice, might best be understood as discriminatory abilities, but it does not really seem to matter whether I am allowed to use the word 'concept' here. These people discriminate between those acts required if social life is to be possible and others, though they discriminate by reference to their taboos and religious precepts rather than by use of a word translatable as 'justice'. They take the taboos as reasons for acting in one way rather than another, and, if the taboos are of the appropriate sort, then they are reasons of justice even though that particular word is not used. This sort of thing is not at all uncommon in our own usage. Rather than using the word 'justice' we frequently say such things as 'It would be murder', 'I promised to', 'I owe it to him', 'It would be wrong', or simply 'I can't do that'. Not everybody who rejects a possible action as unfair, unjust or wrong is capable of articulating the reasons why it is unfair, unjust, or wrong, but that does not mean that he is not exercising a sense of justice or even that he is not employing a concept of justice. One need not be particularly articulate in order to have a sense of justice. Whether we could form a coherent and detailed conception of justice from an examination of taboos such as those described is a separate question, and probably one that needs to be argued out in terms of specific examples.

The objection might be taken further. In order to be just, one must try to be just; simply reacting spontaneously to a situation and doing what is in fact just is not enough. If, as a spontaneous reaction to relieve an old lady's distress, I give her money, with no thought of the fact that I owe her the money and had promised to pay the debt at that time, then I do what is in fact just, but the virtue that I display, if any, is kindness. My forgetfulness shows a want in me meaning that I have not displayed the virtue of justice. If a language has no word translatable as 'justice' and its people simply act in accordance with an appropriate set of taboos, how can they be aiming at justice, or acting for reasons of justice, or displaying a sense of justice?

These people perform a given act because it is required or refrain from a given act because it is forbidden. With their relative lack of sophistication they cannot set out the reasons why the acts are required or forbidden, but that is a lack of sophistication that they share with many people in most societies, and I argued earlier that an ability to set out the reasons is not necessary to a display of a sense of justice. These people act deliberately because the acts are required or prohibited, aiming at meeting the standard set, and the discriminatory function of the requirements and prohibitions is that of the concept of justice. What they lack is the ability to articulate the reasons for the requirements, and that is an ability they need not have. One may need to aim at justice in order to be just, but one need not aim at justice in those words. A man shows no lack of justice if he hands over money because he owes it rather than because justice requires it of him even if he cannot go on to provide a set of reasons why debts should be paid beyond saying that it would be wrong not to pay them. Similarly, the people who deliberately act to satisfy standards which have the function of the concept of justice meet the requirements of my argument.

Co-operative enterprises involve different sorts of reasons which we might distinguish as *reasons inside* and *reasons for* the enterprise. We saw earlier the role that reasons for justice play: they provide reasons inside a co-operative enterprise. Once somebody has entered a co-operative enterprise and taken on a role in it, claims of justice can be made on him and they provide him with reasons for acting. The fact that it is my turn to do the washing up is a reason for me to do the washing up; each of us taking his turn is a necessary condition for the effectiveness of our co-operation in doing the housework. But these points provide somebody with reasons only after he has entered a co-operative enterprise and do nothing at all to provide him with reasons for entering the co-operative enterprise in the first place. Reasons inside the enterprise are not reasons for the enterprise. If a group of us are co-operating in setting up a golf course, then, given the appropriate role in the group, I have a reason for tending the greens, because if that job is not done the co-operation cannot achieve its ends; somebody else will have to do that job as extra work, and it is unjust of me to refuse to do my share if I am going to claim a share of the benefits. But the fact that somebody must take care of the greens if the co-operation is to be effective gives me no reason whatsoever to join the group if I am not already a member. My reasons for joining the group would be different: that I wanted to play golf, that I wanted a share of the profits, or something of that sort. These are not reasons of justice, but they give the co-operation its point and make it worthwhile. Only after I join in an enterprise for some such reason as this do reasons of justice get a grip on me.

The reasons for going into a co-operative enterprise need not be reasons of self-interest. A group of people might co-operate in an attempt to stamp out cruelty to animals, or to provide an ambulance- or fire-service in a community lacking one, and there is no reason to believe that people who do such things are always guilty of self-seeking. At least on the face of it, they are admirably motivated and act out of a wholesome concern for others. One might even institute or join in a co-operative enterprise for reasons of justice, the enterprise itself then being located within a wider context of co-operation. One might, for example, co-operate with others in order to press for the introduction of trial by jury in a legal system without it or to fight the injustices of racial discrimination. The reasons for entering a co-operative enterprise, what determines whether the enterprise is worthwhile or justified, can be of different sorts. What seems clear is that they are distinct from the reasons for doing something inside the enterprise, even if in both cases they are reasons of justice. If I am inside an enterprise then I am subject to its regulations and what is necessary if it is to achieve its end, but the setting up of a golf club is not justified simply by the fact that it is co-operative. Nor is the setting up of a chapter of the Ku Klux Klan or a robber band. They may be co-operative, but they are in a wider and more basic context of co-operation which enables us to say that the reasons for setting them up are unjust and the enterprises are unjustified.

So there are the reasons inside a co-operative enterprise, determined by what is necessary if the enterprise is to achieve its goal, and there are the reasons for entering the enterprise, which are concerned with whether the goal is worthwhile to the person considering whether to enter. This suggests that the reasons of justice inside the enterprise are merely shorthand for, or particular applications of, the reasons for entering the enterprise. Those reasons may be concerned with self-interest or with other things, but they at least have the appearance of being prior to and more basic than the reasons of justice inside the enterprise.

Sometimes there are no reasons for which one entered a co-operative enterprise, because sometimes one simply finds oneself in an enterprise without having chosen or decided to enter it. Most families are more or less co-operative, and as one grows one simply finds oneself in a family without ever having considered whether or not to be a member of it or having chosen to be one. In such a case we cannot contrast a person's reasons for entering the enterprise with the reasons he has for doing certain things within the enterprise, but we can still ask questions about whether it is worth his while to stay in the enterprise. The eldest son might have the job of washing up each night, and it might be quite proper that this task be required of him while he remains a member of the family and accepts the benefits it offers, but one might still properly ask whether he should remain a member of the family if by leaving it he can do better for himself or can ease the lots of thousands in a far-off leper colony. Questions about the reasons for remaining in the enterprise, or whether the enterprise is worthwhile or justified, can still be separated from questions about the reasons for doing certain things inside the enterprise.

So reasons of justice, which arise inside co-operative enterprises, appear to be subject to the reasons which justify the co-operative enterprise by showing that setting it up or retaining it is worthwhile. These reasons may be matters of self-interest, or they may be reasons of another sort. What sort of reasons they are would simply depend on what sort of reason appealed to the person in question, the person of whom we ask whether the enterprise is worth his while. Moral reasons have no special place. Crudely, reasons of justice gain purchase only because co-operation pays. Somebody might say, without logical confusion, that co-operation never pays or helps one to achieve one's ends, so that justice never provides a reason for acting. Anybody who thinks that it does is either mistaken about whether co-operation pays or is confused about the relation between reasons of justice and reasons for co-operating in the first place.

As a development of this objection, somebody might accept the argument that I have produced about the priority of justice but dispute its conclusion, saying that the argument provides us with no more than a chronological story. Perhaps, he might say, we can become rational only through social life and co-operation, with the acceptance of reasons of justice that they require, but having become rational we can look back and see that it would be better never to have co-operated. We can see that co-operation does not pay, so we see that it would be better for us not to co-operate now. People (or rational beings) and rationality will die out with this generation because force provides the only way of resolving disputes, but the rational individual's response to the end of the species with his own demise might be one of indifference. Co-operation is simply an instrument enabling the individual to achieve his own ends, whatever they might be, self-interested or otherwise. Once he became a rational being, he might see that the state of nature was better.

The objection is a forceful and persuasive one, but it is not as clear as might seem that it is successful. It is not really clear that co-operation is *simply* an instrument for gaining one's own ends. Certainly co-operation frequently, even usually, takes on that aspect. I co-operate with others in providing an ambulance service because I may need it or others I care for may need it. But such specific forms of co-operation take place against a background of more general co-operation. Co-operation as such is not simply a means of achieving one's ends; it is also necessary if one is to have or form those ends in the first place. And if co-operation plays the role of putting us in a position to work out what is worthwhile and what is not, it is not clear how co-operation as such, rather than some particular co-operative enterprises, could turn out never to pay. The points raised in the objection seem to be true of most forms of co-operation, but not of that co-operation which is crucial for the argument. Means-end justification seems quite inappropriate in that case.

If reasoning presupposes co-operation, then we cannot subject that form of co-operation to questions of means-end justification. It is simply presupposed; we simply find ourselves in that sort of co-operation with nothing we can do about it and no questions of justification that can properly be raised. The only way in which such co-operation could fail to pay would be if it were better if one had never been born.

Somebody might, on reflection, decide that co-operation paid him so little that it would have been better had he never been born, but the alternative he considers is one of never having existed, not one of having existed without any co-operation. The point of what he says is not to show that reasons of justice have no force or are irrelevant for him but, if he is right about its being better had he never been born, to show that these reasons allow him enormous freedom of action. His claim is that he bears enormous burdens and gains few benefits, so that few claims can properly be made on him. The claims that could be made on him because of the benefits he took have already been met because of the burdens he has borne. Reasons of self-interest are not taking precedence over reasons of justice for this man. Rather, he has an argument of justice to show that, in this situation, justice requires very little of him and allows him to do pretty much as he pleases.

But what of the man who wants to go further: the man who says that a Hobbesian state of nature is the best that we can have? We could not have attained our present state of rationality without co-operation, he might say, but that co-operation has now served its purpose and can be set aside. With the benefit of rationality we can now see that no co-operation is worth the effort, that communal life should be forgotten, and that we should live as in a Hobbesian state of nature. A sensible man should reject all obligations, be prepared to benefit from others if he can, and harm them if he sees fit. If we take this line, then rational life will disappear with this generation, but that is the rational thing for it to do.

The claim that co-operation never pays is plainly false, but pointing that out is not sufficient to refute the objection. The objection may be false, but as long as it is conceivable it serves to make its point: reasons of justice cannot be basic, because they arise only in a co-operative situation, and, if no co-operation pays, then the rational thing to do might be to avoid co-operation. If all co-operation is unjustified, then the reasons of justice within co-operative enterprises are merely apparent; the point that made them reasons is lost if the enterprises are unjustified. So justice never really provides any reason at all. As long as all this is conceivable, whether or not it is true, it follows that reasons of justice are not basic. Even where it is obvious that justice provides reasons, that is only because it is obvious that co-operation pays and therefore obvious that requirements of self-interest are met.

Avoiding co-operation with each other does not mean simply that we set up no golf clubs and have no co-op grocery stores. Rather, it removes all we have that keeps us from a Hobbesian state of nature. We have in our various forms of communal life many co-operative enterprises assigning us roles with their concomitant rights and duties, and all of those would be set aside. There would be no more families, with specified adults assigned the jobs of raising children. There would be no more mutual forbearances for the good of each, and so no recognition of any distinction between mine and thine and also no security against attack from others whenever one might get in their way. With no mutual forbearances, there would be no accepted ways of peaceably settling clashes of interests. People could help me only by accident; they could hinder me simply by going about their own business. On the face of it, simply having other people around is contrary to my interests if we cannot co-operate, and that is part of the nature of this Hobbesian condition to which we should have been reduced. I should, therefore, do something about it. I might remove myself from the scene and set up cave as a hermit. If I do not go away, then I should drive others away or kill them. The same holds true for each of them and the attitude that they should take to the world. We should have no security in our lives, and no possessions, even to the point of not knowing, as we took one mouthful, where the next one was coming from. Life in a state of nature, if it was not solitary, would be poor, nasty, brutish, and extremely short. We should have a genuine fight to the death with each against all, and, with such odds against each one, nobody could be a good bet to win. Choosing this option, as far as the probabilities go, would be, for each man, tantamount to choosing suicide. The rationality of suicide is not something that I want to discuss here, nor is it something that I need to. Certainly one can be unjust in committing suicide; one can leave one's children uncared for and a burden on others, debts unpaid, and so on. What one cannot do by committing suicide, is remove oneself from the influence of considerations of justice and leave oneself to be properly guided only by reasons of self-interest. The dead are not touched by any reasons.

It might seem that my argument here has not gone far enough; it may be true that, for each person, the chances of beating everybody else in a fight are negligible, but it is surely still a logical possibility that somebody be strong and tough enough to do so. It is obvious that nobody could actually do so, but no more obvious than it is that co-operation pays, so this is a mere matter of fact that cannot properly be used in the argument at this stage.

Whether a statement is a mere matter of fact is not determined simply by applying tests to its logical form. One point that can affect the status of the statement is the sort of circumstances required to give point to the concepts employed, and that matters in this case. Morality has its home in relations between people, and these relations give morality its point. Morality has no place in relations between Kantian gods or between beasts. A being strong enough to win the fight against everybody else, never sleeping and invulnerable to concerted attack from all others, is not a person; his needs and interests are not human needs and interests, and his predicament is not the human predicament that gives point to so many of our practical concepts. Moral concepts have no place in his world, so he cannot be used to set up a contrast between moral and self-interested reasons and to show that self-interested reasons come out on top. He does not affect claims about the human world. Our relations with a being such as the one described would be analogous in many respects to our relations with beasts.

So it is not as clear as it might seem that a human world in which co-operation never paid is conceivable. It appears that we might be conceiving oblivion instead. The nearest we can get to that in a situation that clearly is conceivable is the case of the hermit, and that is not sufficient to show reasons of self-interest to be prior to reasons of justice. The hermit has simply placed himself in a position in which justice will, in fact, require very little of him.

It does seem clear that, with most co-operative enterprises, we can ask whether it is worth our while to join them and make ourselves subject to the claims of justice generated within them, but it is not obvious that this shows a dependence of reasons of justice on reasons of self-interest or what sort of dependence it might show. The dependence is not chronological. It is not that our becoming subject to claims within a co-operative enterprise is always a matter of our decision or consideration of reasons. Sometimes we simply find ourselves in one as we grow. Nor does there seem to be a logical dependence in particular cases. If I miscalculate, so that I join in an enterprise expecting to gain a benefit which, in the end, is not forthcoming, that fact does not seem to release me from my obligations. If we set up a business, agreeing to share the profits and the costs fifty-fifty, the fact that the business failed to make a profit would not normally be regarded as releasing me from my obligation to pay half the costs. And it is not clear that there could be a dependence in general, either, since, as we have seen, our being able to ask of particular enterprises whether they are worth our while or serve our interests is itself dependent on co-operation at another level.

Certainly justice and self-interest are not unrelated. Justice pays; each of us benefits from being in a world of justice rather than a world of chaos, and that is one of the reasons it is important that we should discriminate in terms of the concept of justice. It is one of the facts giving point to the concept of justice. But the point of a concept is not one of its elements, and justice is not merely shorthand for reasons of self-interest. Possession of Gyges' ring would not ease the restrictions on a just man. And for the same reason, self-interest could not lead us to be just. If it led us there it could lead us elsewhere, and it would do so whenever justice and long-term self-interest clashed. If it is a question of where self-interest leads us, then methods of discovering infractions and enforcing regulations are of prime importance. Self-interest might lead us to set up a state and police force, but it could not lead us to be just men. Justice, in such a situation, would be reduced to the edicts of the state.

My argument remains, then, that reasons of justice are basic to rationality. Somebody who says that self-interest provides reasons but justice is only a matter of confused sentimentality is in a self-defeating position. What makes reasons of self-interest reasons also makes reasons of justice reasons, and more important ones.

It does not follow, and is not intended to follow, from my argument that everything is just. Though people have a sense of justice, care about justice, and accept ever so cheerfully that considerations of justice constitute reasons for acting, there may be many ways in which things can go wrong and injustices appear. People may make mistakes of fact, such as believing that some particular skin-colour betokens inferiority, or, given that they are right and in agreement about the facts, they might still make mistakes in their calculations. The circumstances in which some moral practice grew up might change so that burdens formerly necessary if some benefit were to be produced need no longer be borne, but an unreflective acceptance of tradition might keep the practice going. There might simply be vice in some people, who want what they can get, regarding the trustingness of others as foolishness and not caring that they are being unreasonable. Or there might be cases of weakness of will. (It is perhaps worth noting that on this account, unlike the account of reasons as facts plus desires, the relation of the reasons to human nature explains both how reasons can be practical and how they can fail to be practical.)

Social life involves disputes, and the sort of question raised in a dispute is, typically, a moral question, often taking a form such as 'Is X blameworthy?'. Where an agreement has been made, for example, then determining what was agreed to is not simply a matter of consulting a dictionary with the written agreement in hand; questions of justification are commonly raised. I agreed to do A, but, as it turns out, doing A in the circumstances at the time amounts to or involves doing B. Is my agreement to do A, an agreement to do only A, which is now impossible, or does the agreement extend? Does my agreement to do A amount to an agreement to do B in the circumstances? Which description applies? The question being raised is one of justification, or of whether I am blameworthy in not doing A, and such questions of justification involve the invocation of moral concepts. I agreed to do the baby-sitting from 7.30, but have I agreed to stop the discussion, miss my dinner, or ignore the fact that my house is burning down? Under what conditions am I justified in being late for the baby-sitting? This sort of question cannot be asked or answered if there is no morality.

My argument here can be read as similar to Hobbes' argument about laws of nature. He argued that his laws of nature were rules people must follow to leave the state of nature; I re-read them as descriptions of qualities of character that people must have if they are not to live in a state of nature now. People must be relatively peaceable, honest, and so on. In short, they must be willing to co-operate. One is tempted to emphasise the point by saying that people must, by the large, have these qualities of character naturally; if they had not, they could not have social life and the reasoning necessary for them to work out the laws of nature as matters of self-interested policy.

We can tell what is a law of nature or a virtue and what is not by seeing whether a certain sort of behaviour or a certain quality of character is necessary for social life. It might be that there are no necessary conditions for social life though many different sufficient conditions, but Hobbes has disposed of that problem in his initial account of human nature: it is, at least, necessary that people not be like that. Since what is necessary for social life must be there, there must be a law of nature even though we may not be sure of its content. If certain sorts of behaviour are necessary for social life, then knowledge of the law of nature as such will not be necessary for it to be efficacious. If certain sorts of behaviour are necessary for social life, then it will be no accident that social beings regard behaviour to the contrary as improper, and it will be no accident that they regard certain facts as reasons for acting, for example, as reasons for restraining somebody, even as reasons for restraining themselves when they have a choice between right and wrong. The importance of their behaving in this manner depends in no way on their understanding why they should do so or why the reasons they accept should be reasons. Here we see, perhaps, some of the appeal of Intuitionism. Unreflective morality will, by and large, do the job[6]. Moral philosophy is not necessary to fulfil the requirements of natural law, nor is a great deal of moral sophistication.

When I claim that certain concepts are presupposed by human life, which I take to be fairly close to Kant's claim that certain concepts are presupposed by experience, I am not, as far as I can tell, committing myself to anything like a theory of innate ideas. I do not deny that we learn the concepts or that we are brought up to behave in certain ways; rather, I assert that it is no accident that we learn these concepts and are brought up to behave in those ways. The claim that people in general must behave in certain ways or operate certain concepts does not seem to commit me to any particular explanation of why they behave in those ways or how they gain the concepts.

Given this account of natural law or the nature of virtues, one can see that reason would reveal it to us: we should discover the content of natural law by thinking, by working out what is necessary for social life. In part of what I said, we can see another connection between reason and natural law: it is a necessary condition of social life that laws of nature provide reasons for acting. Laws of nature will be practical requirements of reason, though not the formal requirements of a formal reason that Kant had in mind.

My argument about justice plainly fits this mould. Co-operation and the operation of a concept of justice are presupposed by social life, so it is no accident that considerations of justice are accepted as reasons for acting: were they not, social life would be impossible, and without social life there could be no reasons. So a condition of anything's being accepted as a reason by anybody is that considerations of justice are by and large accepted as reasons.

If we talk of treating something as a reason, that would

normally suggest a claim much weaker than the one I am making. It brings to mind examples such as 'If you say that the government is less than perfect, it will treat that as a reason for locking you up'. This suggests that the government will treat your opinion *as though* it were a reason for locking you up, with the implication that it is not really such a reason. 'We treat them as reasons' suggests 'but they might not really be', or at least it suggests that we might just as well treat other things as reasons instead. My argument is intended to rule these replies out; it is intended to show that these things are and must be reasons, that it is no accident that we treat them as such. It is certainly intended to show more than that we *simply* treat these things as reasons, and if anybody should accept the argument but say that that is all it shows, then I shall ask him to explain what more it would be for something to *be* a reason.

That considerations of justice are reasons is a presupposition of social life and of all reasoning, so a man has reasons to be moral if he has reason for anything. Accepting moral reasons as the most important sort of reasons for acting is different from accepting as such facts about the day of the week, the colours of flowers, or the welfare of trees, and giving precedence to people over trees is not arbitrary.

It follows from my argument, further, that moral reasons are overriding, that is, that they take precedence over other sorts of reasons. This is not the pointless claim that morality gives moral reasons precedence over others, nor is it the similar psychological claim that people will always give them preference. It is the logical or conceptual claim that non-moral reasons are dependent on a conceptual frame which has moral reasons as its base. And this is not simply a claim about *our* conceptual frame; if my argument is correct, it is correct for any human life and thus for any conceptual frame. Those philosophical positions taking self-interest as the paradigm of a reason for acting and as basic are therefore false; that considerations of self-interest can provide reasons for acting presupposes that considerations of justice provide reasons for acting, that is, it is dependent on justice as providing reasons. One cannot, therefore, rationally prefer reasons of self-interest to reasons of justice, because there can be such reasons only within a conceptual framework putting reasons of justice at the base. Social life is comprehensible only in terms of the concept of justice.

This argument about the fundamental role of justice is intended to show that moral considerations are, quite objectively, reasons, and that it is, therefore, rational to be just. It is not an attempt to give further self-interested reasons for accepting moral reasons, viz. that the Fabric of Society will collapse if one does not do the Right. One person's actions by themselves probably have a negligible effect on the Fabric of Society. Nor is the argument the Baierian one[7] that there is a self-interested reason for choosing to accept moral reasons, viz. that each of us is better off if we have a system overriding reasons of self-interest at various times. Baier might explain why *we* should accept moral reasons if all of us must be the same, but he does not explain why *I* should accept moral reasons. If all of us must be the same then we might have a choice only between morality and a free for all, but I have a further alternative; I can try to trick everybody else into being moral and myself remain devoted to my own interests alone.

This does not mean that morality is in no way related to self-interest, but the concepts are not self-interest concepts: the relation to self-interest is not one of the elements of the concepts. Being just may be good for me, but being just does not *mean* doing what is good for me and there is no paradox involved when I find a case in which my being just is contrary to my interests. Clever but completely self-interested men would not form moral concepts, but that story does not give an analysis of the concepts anyway. The story of clever, self-interested men bargaining could be no more than speculative history about how men came to make certain institutional arrangements, and speculative history involving all the traditional problems of Hobbes' state of nature. If moral concepts are treated as though they were formed by some one man on his own rather than inter-personally, or if self-interest is given as the underlying reason why the concept or what is brought under it matters, then self-interest becomes the form of the concept — as we saw earlier, it changes the concept, the action required, and the consequences[8]. Moral concepts could never then require that a man act in a way not in his overall interests. Each man working for his own good individually need not be, and is not, the same as social men working to get what is the best possible for each.

Again, my argument does not show that justice bears no relation to the consequences of actions. It is the consequences of our having a concept of justice that make it so important and give the concept the point it has, but that does not mean that justice is a consequentialist concept and that the justice of any action or distribution has to be worked out in terms of its consequences as Utilitarianism proposes. The consequences of our having a concept of justice inform the concept, but are not elements of it. They are why we classify things in terms of certain characteristics, but they are not themselves the characteristics. As a consequence of having the concept of justice we are able to classify things in certain ways that are of crucial importance to us. As a consequence of having the concept of repair we are able to classify things in certain ways that are important to us, but the concept of repair is also a consequentialist concept: the test of whether something has been repaired is the consequences of our tinkering. Consequences are important to the concept of justice because they provide its point, but *justice* is not a consequentialist concept as *repair* is.

The particular consequences that are of crucial importance in the case of the concept of justice are that it makes possible social or human life, so the account that I have been setting out does bear some resemblance to an evolutionary theory of ethics, at least insofar as it suggests that a book such as Darwin's *Descent of Man* ought to provide food for a moral philosopher's thought. My claim is not, though, that 'good' means 'furthering evolution'. The point that I made above about consequences in general applies also to this specific sort of consequence. The context of social life and interaction explains why certain concepts are forced on us and it informs those concepts, but it is not one of the elements of those concepts. We must have a concept of murder because social life requires that we have one, but that requirement does not mean that what is wrong with a case of murder is that it interferes with evolution. If I dispatch my 60 year-old mother-in-law, evolution will probably not be affected at all. What is wrong with murder is that it is murder and, as such, unjust. The role of social life or of evolution is to explain the importance and point of the concept, not the morality of the act.

What happens, then, when I meet a self-interested man who 'hard-headedly' asks why he should care about moral considerations? I go through the argument and give him the reasons, but doing that need neither move him nor convince him. That he has been neither moved nor convinced does not mean that his question has not been answered. It might mean that he ought to be locked up, but that is a different matter. He may not contradict himself, but if he says that he is reasonable in being completely self-interested, then he is committed to reasons and the structure thereof. Since reasoning and, therefore, reasons of self-interest, presuppose reasons of justice, he is committed to accepting, and not rejecting, moral reasons.

It is not that the self-interested man has no reasons or is failing to reason at all. The moves he makes are recognisable as reasoning because, in a different context in which they did not clash with reasons of justice, his points would constitute good reasons. Because they are in conflict with reasons of justice, it follows that they are bad reasons. The mistake that he makes is not the fairly unusual one of contradicting himself, but that he flies against one of the presuppositions of what he is doing.

NOTES

1   A.I. Melden, *Free Action* (Routledge and Kegan Paul, London, 1961), pp.146–7.
2   P.H. Nowell-Smith, *Ethics* (Pelican, Harmondsworth, 1954), p.114.
3   *Ibid*. p.120.
4   *Ibid*. p.120.
5   Hume, *Treatise of Human Nature*, ed. Selby-Bigge (Oxford, 1888), p.494.
6   This point is reflected in the work of sociobiologists. See, for example, Edward O. Wilson, *On Human Nature*, (Harvard University Press, Cambridge, Massachusetts, and London, England, 1978).
7   Kurt Baier, *The Moral Point of View* (Cornell University Press, Ithaca, N.Y., 1958), chapter 12.

8   It is easy to make this mistake of treating the point of the concept as though it were one of the elements of the concept. Edward O. Wilson seems to make the mistake in *On Human Nature* (Harvard University Press, Cambridge, Massachusetts, and London, England, 1978), especially in chapter 7 when he argues about '. . . the ultimately self-serving quality of most forms of [human] altruism'.

SEVEN
Virtues

The previous argument about the role of a sense of justice in our lives as rational beings underlines also the central role that justice plays in morality. When we are faced with a question about what we ought to do, justice imposes requirements on us, and it is a presupposition of our rational and human life that those requirements be given rational precedence over everything else. Not all questions about what we ought to do are to be settled in terms of justice, because the function of justice is the negative one of ruling out some possible actions and requiring that they not be done rather than the positive one of requiring that some specific act be done. Justice allocates rights or claims and requires that they not be infringed, but it does not require that the person who has the right or claim should press it and insist on having what is his. Should he want to, he can (provided that he infringes nobody else's rights) share it, give it away, or ignore it. Given that justice allows a range of possible courses of action in a given case, we can still ask, of actions within that range, which we ought to do. The reasons why I ought to do whatever it is are not of the same sort as those involved in an issue of justice, and it is not that sort of requirement that is expressed; the English word 'ought' covers a multitude of virtues and more than one relation. One might, jumping the gun just a little, express the difference in this case by saying that the other virtues give good reasons for acting, whereas justice gives compelling reasons.

Given that justice allows a range of possible courses of action, we can still ask, of actions within that range, which we ought to do, and the question will be answered by reference to notions other than justice. I can, perhaps, quite justly insist that you keep a promise that both of us now realise you were foolish to make, but might it not be cruel of me to do so? Or might it not be imprudent of me to do so? Without having any specific rights against anybody else, I might be at liberty (within the normal limits) to do whatever I want on a spring day, but might it not be kinder to visit my aged and lonely aunt than to spend the time reading in a hammock? It might be concluded that I ought to release you from your promise and ought to visit my aunt (if one wants to, one could say that I morally ought to do those two things), but the situations are not ones with a morality of strict requirement as they would be were they issues of justice. They are, nevertheless, proper questions about what I ought to do, and questions which can be plausibly described as moral. They introduce virtues other than justice. There is more to morality than justice, and more to living a human life than merely getting by.

Human life, I have argued, presupposes that people by and large have a sense of justice, but that requirement about the virtue of justice is a minimal one: it would be a remarkably unpleasant life if people were no better than they ought to be or could be required to be in terms of justice. A world in which each man simply gave what was due from him and insisted on what was due to him would be a harsh and cold world with no mercy, kindness, or forgiveness. We could, no doubt, live in such a world, but it would not be much fun. It is no accident that, by and large, we try to bring our children up to be just, because bringing up would stop, and would have stopped already, if it were otherwise. In a weaker way, it is no accident that we try to bring our children up to be kind, brave, considerate, prudent, and so on. A sense of justice may be necessary, but the other virtues have their place. The sense of justice makes human life possible, and the other virtues make it worthwhile. My argument earlier was that social or human life involved willingness to co-operate and therefore, specifically, a sense of justice, but it also involves some interest in and warm feeling for other people and hence, in a general way, other virtues.

The sense of justice comes into play when we co-operate, but a simple willingness to meet proper claims will not explain how co-operation ever began. As for that, there must be the warmer feelings involved in willingness to co-operate. People must be approachable and ready to approach others.

It is only within the context of life's being possible that it can be worthwhile, and it is only within a context of justice that the other virtues come into play. Justice sets the range of morally possible actions, and within that range the other virtues pick out the act to be performed. Justice makes the harsh imposition of requirements, and what justice dictates may be demanded of me as kindness may not be. If kindness could be demanded of me as justice can, then it should no more give rise to gratitude than should a routine payment of debts (which is not to suggest that courtesy is out of place in a routine payment of debts). Gratitude is an appropriate response to acts of kindness because they cannot be required as justice can; paying for the bread I buy is not at all the same thing as giving the same amount of money to somebody else so that he can use it to pursue his pleasure even though he has no claim on it. Not being kind, then, is a different fault, and a different kind of fault, from not being just. It warrants a different response, and, because of the different roles played in our social life by justice and kindness, it warrants a less stringent response.

The relationships between virtues and vices in their general outline are similar to the structure of Islaamic law. At the centre we have matters of requirement or prohibition, which are issues of justice. In these cases we have rights, and demands can be made, though whether we choose to exercise a given right is a separate question. It is with cases in this area that justified coercion will have its home, backing up the demands which must be met, though there are many reasons why not every claim should be backed by coercion: the possibility that a mistake has been made in working out the rights, the possibility in some cases that coercion would cause more trouble than it is worth, and so on. Alongside these matters of requirement or prohibition we have matters of complete indifference, such as (other things being equal) whether I boil the cabbage for five minutes or ten when cooking my dinner. Then we have cases of action that is not required but is praiseworthy, and it is here that the other virtues appear. If you are not my teacher or anything of the sort then I may not be able to require that you spend any of your time on me, but it might be praiseworthy if you did so as an act of kindness. Lastly, we have acts which are not prohibited but are frowned upon, and it is here that vices other than injustice have their place. If you lose to me in a poker game then you owe me the money. I can properly assert my right to it, am not prohibited from doing so, though it might be cruel for me to do so if I knew that paying the debt would preclude your buying an anniversary present for your wife and would cause you untold trouble.

A comment should be interpolated here about my description of the general relationship between virtues and vices, because the notion of what is praiseworthy might be misleading. Despite what that notion might suggest, simply doing what is required of one and never doing anything that is praiseworthy is not perfectly satisfactory or par for the course. Never doing anything that is praiseworthy is itself to be frowned upon; simply failing to exhibit a particular virtue such as kindness in some circumstances can amount to exhibiting a vice such as callousness. Some situations leave me no choice about revealing my moral character. That simply failing to be praiseworthy can itself properly be frowned upon shows that the notion of what is praiseworthy has been distorted, but I can find no better word. Nevertheless, given this proviso, any particular act will fall into one of the categories of the neutral, the required, the prohibited, the praiseworthy, and the frowned upon.

Virtues and vices can be divided up in a number of different ways. They are fairly commonly divided in terms of whether they are self-regarding or other-regarding. They can be divided up in terms of whether I must aim at them to exhibit them: if I am not trying to be just, under that description, then the justice of my act is accidental and I do not exhibit the virtue of justice; if I do aim to be kind, under that description, rather than, say, to help Bill, then it is at least arguable that I am not actually kind though I might be conscientious or exhibit some other virtue; it is, perhaps, possible to be prudent whether one aims at that virtue or not. These different divisions of virtues and vices are not incompatible with each other, and the particular division that I have set out above could be refined a good deal. It is not intended to be the only one or to be definitive. It is intended only to be sufficient to my purposes.

A virtue is a property that gets something done; 'virtue' is a term concerned with means, and it makes sense only when ends have been set. What is a virtue may, therefore, vary from case to case. The nearest anything can come to being simply a virtue whatever may occur will be if there are certain inescapable ends; in the same way that I have argued that inter-personal or communal life is an inescapable end because of the role it plays in giving sense to the idea of reasoning. One of the virtues of a diamond is that it is hard, but hardness is no virtue in my pillow. Diamonds and pillows are put to quite different uses, and the properties in each which will make it more efficiently serve its purposes are different. What makes hardness a virtue in diamonds are the uses to which diamonds are put and the fact that hardness helps in achieving those ends. Things which, apparently, have no purpose in the relevant way take on virtues and vices in a similar fashion. That it runs for thousands of miles is a virtue in a car, but not in an infant I must care for while working. The infant is not an instrument of mine as is the car, but he does, nevertheless, affect the efficiency with which I can achieve my purposes, and that assessment of the infant is one quite plainly made considering him in those terms. If we omitted reference to my having to care for the child while working and simply asked for virtues in a child, lack if liveliness would probably not appear on the list. Children, though, are often assessed in terms of the interests of adults because they are not adults and are assumed not to have developed the rational capacities involved in having at least most of the human virtues. Adults, not infants, are paradigmatic people. A good baby is one who sleeps right through the night, not one who helps the needy.

The idea of a virtue as a power or efficacy is fairly plainly the primary one. The other main sense noted by the *Oxford English Dictionary* is that of virtue as conforming one's life to moral principles. This second sense, in which the word does not take a plural, is probably best understood in terms of the other: a life of virtue can be understood in terms of a life exhibiting virtues, though the two seem by no means to be exactly the same. A life of virtue suggests something fairly self-conscious and probably rule bound, whereas some of the virtues involve an unselfconscious spontaneity of feeling and action. A life of virtue, as that phrase is normally used, might be one of propriety and fulfilment of just duties rather than one of friendship and warm kindness, but it is difficult to understand the notion at all if it does not involve reference to some virtues, and those virtues can be understood as powers. The ends involved, those that I have argued are inescapable in human life, will explain which powers are virtues and why they are virtues.

Human life, as we have seen, makes presuppositions about human nature, and what it presupposes about human nature is concerned with virtues and vices. Moral philosophy consists largely of the development of an account of human nature. Reasoning, one of the important points distinguishing us from mere brutes, requires interpersonal or communal life, and we can have such life only if people by and large exhibit such propensities as a willingness to help each other from time to time without requirement or expectation of return. It is no accident or mere matter of decision, therefore, that these propensities are encouraged and are to be encouraged. They are human or social virtues, serving ends forced upon us by human life, and that they are such virtues is a matter of the human condition.

A communal life is one lived co-operatively with others, and simply the fact that it is that sort of thing determines in a number of respects what is a better social life and what worse. Co-operation, as we saw earlier, is not something that is simply either present or absent, but admits of degrees. An activity can be more or less co-operative. And co-operation can be more or less efficient and more or less easy and congenial or uneasy and felt as a burden. These points give us criteria within the notion of communal life itself for what will be a better communal life and what will be a worse one, as such. Many extraneous judgments can be made about many ways of living communally, but some judgments are shown to be relevant, not by considerations outside the particular way of living communally, as a commune-seeker might decide that a particular commune would not suit his purposes, but by the notion of communal life itself. A sense of justice is a necessary condition of communal life. Communal life being what it is, properties that make it more efficient or more congenial will be virtues. Properties that make it less efficient or less congenial will be vices.

If I am to co-operate with a man, then there are many things that I might reasonably want to know about him simply in terms of the possibility and effectiveness of co-operative action with him. I shall need to have some idea of how strong his sense of justice is, because if it is not strong enough, or if he is too weak-willed, then co-operative enterprise with him will be impossible. A failure to consider his share of the work and the benefits, or constant attempts to take more than his share of the benefits and do less than his share of the work, would make the co-operative enterprise with him pointless and inoperable. If the enterprise were a large one and he only a small part of it, then the enterprise might survive his defalcations, but then he would not be a proper part of the co-operation between members.

I might also reasonably want to know how kind a man is, how willing to do things simply to help even when those things are not part of his job in the enterprise and cannot be required of him. A man who will always insist on his rights, doing what can be required of him and refusing to do any more, never pointing out that the tester has missed a crucial sample or showing Sam where the monkey-wrench was left, makes the whole enterprise less efficient. If he never encourages anybody despite their mistakes, but always condemns, he will make the enterprise both less efficient and less congenial. On the other hand, if he goes too far, always interfering and overseeing others' jobs, doing everything for them and never leaving them alone, he will equally surely make the enterprise less congenial and therefore less efficient. By making others put up with such irritation he is, in effect, increasing their workload. He is, at least, in a general sense, increasing the burdens that they must bear in order to produce the benefits of the enterprise.

The same point holds over a wider range for any particular enterprise. The man who can leave nobody's business alone but is always prying into the private lives of others is a burden to be borne along with the tilling of the soil and the sowing of the seed; he therefore detracts from the ease with which the enterprise might be carried on. Equally, the man with no sympathy for his fellow-workers makes the enterprise a worse one than it might have been. The man who will not overlook some lapses from a colleague and help him out even though he knows that the colleague is recently bereaved or is currently, on a rare occasion, simply suffering from a hangover, is a less than ideal member of a co-operative enterprise. There is a mean to be found between culpable interference and treating people as though they were no more than their jobs in the enterprise, and how well a man exhibits that mean affects how well he can co-operate.

Kindness and consideration are virtues in a co-operative enterprise because of what a co-operative enterprise is; we determine that they are virtues there by considering what a co-operative enterprise is and not by measuring the enterprise against some separate standard. They are means: we can have too much or too little of the propensities which, in the right amount, constitute kindness and consideration. What that mean is, or what the right amount is, is determined by effects on the co-operation. Communal or social life, the presupposition of rational or human life, is itself co-operative, so kindness and consideration are virtues in people and not simply on the production line.

One can see, then, that it is no matter of accident or mere whim that kindness and consideration are encouraged and should be encouraged. That they are virtues and should be encouraged follows from the co-operative basis of human life. The point is not as tight a one as it is in the case of justice, since that deals with a necessary condition, but it follows in the same sort of way that kindness and consideration, though not necessary conditions, are very desirable conditions, worthy of our attention and encouragement. Similar sorts of points follow about reasons which are concerned with kindness or consideration. They are not compelling or over-riding reasons, as are reasons of justice, to be given precedence over all others, but they necessarily are good reasons: the role that they play in the co-operative life that is presupposed by reasoning guarantees them that. That somebody is ill is a reason for helping him. Not all facts are simply neutral between actions, and not all reasons call on the wants of the particular agent. It matters, of course, whether somebody better qualified to help is available (the best way for me to help might be by fetching the doctor), whether my helping the sick man means that I must fail to perform other duties, whether he has meningitis or a headache, whether his headache is a result of self-indulgence last night or of my (accidentally or deliberately) dropping a flower pot on his head, and so on, but, other things being equal, his being ill is a reason for my helping him whether I want to or not. Reasons, coming from an inter-personal background, can conflict with my personal wants and thus create the tension that Kant thought was reflected in the notion of duty.

Reasons of justice take precedence over all others including reasons of kindness, so, in that respect, kindness is limited by justice. Reasons of kindness have force only within the boundaries of what is allowed by justice and are overridden whenever they come in conflict with justice. We have already seen in our discussions of justice and kindness that the fact that they are virtues is intimately related to their providing reasons: their being virtues and their providing reasons are merely different facets of the same things, the role that each plays in human life. As reasons of kindness are subject to and limited by reasons of justice, so the virtue of kindness is subject to and limited by justice. The propensity which, in the appropriate degree, constitutes the virtue of kindness might, in excess of that degree, lead a man to help somebody in ways that are unjust to somebody else, but his help is not then an instance of kindness. Kindness is a mean, and he has not found the mean. He has, in one sense, the same sort of quality of character as the kind man, responding to the wants and interests of others, but he is partial. The father who goes without something himself to give his child enormous pleasure by providing him with an electric train or a holiday on a farm has not refused to recognise any claims of justice but has only refused to press his own; he has not been unjust, but has been kind and thoroughly admirable. The father who, on the other hand, provides one child with a train or a holiday only at the expense of keeping another on short rations, with no special story to explain the preference, can be described, at best, as confusedly kind. He may have the same sort of quality of character as the kind man, but it does not constitute the virtue of kindness because it lacks the point that makes kindness a virtue. His willingness to ignore the rights of some in order to help others shows that his attitude to the situation lacks the required point. He may have

the feelings of warmth towards somebody also appropriate to
a kind man, but those feelings lack the appropriate intellectual
structure. It might be said that, since he is confusedly kind, he is still
kind, but 'A is an XY' does not always entail 'A is a Y', even
though there is usually some fairly obvious equivocation.
That Macbeth held an imaginary dagger could not be a proper
basis for a case against him for possession of a dangerous
weapon, even though daggers were dangerous weapons. A
counterfeit Vermeer is not a Vermeer. From the fact that
somebody is confusedly kind we cannot immediately
conclude that he is kind, but must rather investigate the nature
of the confusion. The second father I described above can be
said to be confusedly *kind* because he does display a warmth of
feeling towards somebody else and a sympathetic response to
their desires, both features appropriate to the kind man, but he
must be described as *confusedly* kind, and not simply as kind,
because he lacks those crucial elements that give to the kind
man the virtue of kindness. If somebody still wants to say that
the father is kind, then so be it, but the kindness he has is not a
virtue, and there does seem some point to restricting the
notion of kindness to the virtue.

Why kindness should be so limited by justice seems fairly
plain in terms of what has been said already. Justice makes
co-operation possible, and kindness is a virtue in that it makes
that co-operation easier and more efficient. If kindness
allowed injustice then, in the extreme case, it would make the
co-operation impossible rather than easier, and in less extreme
cases, which do not cause the collapse of the enterprise, it
would make the job of patching up the activity and keeping it
going more difficult rather than easier and more efficient, so
that it would not be a virtue. This is something to do with the
point of the concept of kindness and what makes it a virtue,
and kindness, of course, shares that point with all the other
virtues. Because of this, the same arguments will apply in the
case of each of the other virtues. Each virtue is limited by and
overridden by considerations of justice and is a virtue only
within the boundaries set by justice. The other virtues will
similarly provide good reasons, though not compelling ones
as justice does.

There are still many other characteristics which are relevant to the effectiveness of co-operation between people in the appropriate ways and which, therefore, constitute virtues or vices. Prudence is one such characteristic. If I were faced with the possibility of co-operating with a man in an important enterprise, one thing I should reasonably want to know about him would be whether he was prudent. By this I do not mean that I should want to know whether he was simply self-seeking, though the term 'prudence' often seems to have that sense today. I should indeed want to know whether he was simply self-seeking, but that comes under a heading other than 'prudence'. What I want to know about him now is whether he has the virtue of prudence, which, like other virtues, is bounded by justice. I want to know whether he is careful, circumspect, and judicious; whether, within what is allowed by his own rights, he takes proper care of his interests. If he is careless of them, then he will be less capable of doing his job and co-operating properly, so that he will throw more of a burden onto the rest of us. Just such an effect on the co-operative enterprise helps to determine what counts as proper care of one's interest and to distinguish kindness from imprudence. One form of imprudence is an excess of the mean that is kindness.

It is not that we determine afterwards whether an act was imprudent or kind by seeing what the consequences are. Whether I am being *careful* of my interests is something that I can know beforehand even if my mistake or some intervening factor makes things go wrong. Being prudent is having proper care for my interests, not always getting things right and producing the desired consequences. The different consequences of the different qualities of character are what make them and the distinction between them important, giving point to the concepts. Such reference to the consequences is not itself part of the concepts of prudence and kindness, and they are not consequentialist concepts as *repair* is. I may be prudent and kind, deciding with proper care for my interests that I can properly give some money to somebody who needs it. The next day, with no reasonable expectation of anything of the sort's happening, I may be shot in the knee-cap on my way to a lecture by a drunken and inaccurate assassin who mistook the man ten yards behind me for the Prime Minister, and because I had given away money I may have difficulty in paying exorbitant medical bills. This unfortunate consequence of my helping another does not show that either I or my act was unkind and imprudent, or even kind but imprudent. To judgments of the kindness and prudence of both my act and me, the consequences of the act are irrelevant. The function of consequences is to show why certain qualities of character are important and to give point to the distinctions we draw between them in our concepts, not to serve as the yardstick by which we should judge particular acts.

In any co-operative enterprise, imprudence is a vice. The man who drinks with no thought of the morrow will fail to clock in or will work inefficiently, increasing the loads of others. The man who, in carefree style, stands drinks for the bar, leaves to others the task of providing him and his dependants with food. The man who smokes heavily and has children to care for had better take out life insurance. Failure to take proper care of one's interests gets in the way of co-operative enterprise and is for that reason a vice.

Charity is a virtue, partly because it stretches what is prudent. A proper risk that will help a co-operative enterprise is more likely to be taken by somebody who knows that he will be cared for if things go wrong, and a willingness to help others to whom one is not (already) co-operatively related is a quality of character which will at least help to get co-operative enterprises off the ground. Loyalty is a virtue, because it is much easier to co-operate with somebody who will stick with it once he has joined in rather than abandon the enterprise and the others involved in it as soon as a better offer comes along for him. Courage is a virtue because it helps to keep an enterprise running properly in the face of danger, protecting against invasion our rights in the life we share with others. And so on.

That list of virtues could no doubt be extended in several ways, but I want to extend it only by mentioning two more virtues which might be of a significantly different type. In a lot of co-operative enterprises and in many aspects of social life, intelligence is a virtue. Superior intelligence will produce the benefits of the enterprise, or will produce them more efficiently than they would otherwise have been produced.

Many of the advances in medicine, which have contributed much to our lives, could not have been made without exceptional intelligence. (Nor, probably, could they have been made without the sort of co-operation that enables some to devote themselves to medical research while others produce food and clothing.) In such cases, intelligence is clearly a virtue.

Similarly, physical strength is often a virtue. Medical research is one useful undertaking, but bringing in the crops is another, and that requires strength. Many of the benefits we acquire through social life can be produced only with the use of great physical strength. In such cases, physical strength is clearly a virtue.

Justice, courage, intelligence, and strength, then, are all human virtues. The problem about listing them together is that many people would want to say that the first two are moral virtues and the last two not, and it is not really clear how that distinction is to be drawn. Nor is it really clear whether it matters how that distinction is drawn, or even whether it matters whether that distinction is drawn. Justice and courage may be moral virtues and strength and intelligence non-moral virtues, but any parent worth his salt will, in bringing up his children, not only try to teach them to be just and brave, but also try to see that they have a proper diet and exercise so that they will be as strong as possible and teach them those intellectual skills that he can. The parent who concentrates only on the moral virtues is not doing his job properly, and in terms of what we should try to develop in ourselves and in others, at least, the distinction between moral and non-moral virtues is not worth making.

One point of the distinction might be, ignoring questions about determinism, that we blame people for not being just but do not blame them for not being strong (unless their not being strong is a matter of imprudence, in which case the complaint is about lack of the virtue of prudence and not about lack of the virtue of strength). More precisely, perhaps, the act of a just man can be performed by an act of will, but a mere act of will does not enable the weakling to perform feats of strength. Justice and courage are matters of my character in a way in which strength and intelligence are not; the moral virtues reflect the agent's intentions and reasons, the sorts of things he tries to do and over the doing of which he has control. Because they are to do with acts over which he has control, exhibitions of moral vice and virtue are matters for which the agent can properly be held responsible. The non-moral virtues are not of that sort, so the point of the distinction between moral and non-moral virtues and vices might well be to do with the propriety of certain judgments and certain responses to exhibitions of those virtues and vices.

Another difference between the two is that moral virtues are always virtues, whereas non-moral virtues are not. Justice, kindness, courage, prudence, and so on are of help in any co-operative endeavour; it was that very point in terms of which I explained why they are virtues. It follows simply from what a co-operative enterprise as such is, that these qualities of character are virtues. Strength and intelligence, on the other hand, are sometimes virtues and sometimes irrelevant. If the enterprise is one of book-keeping, then great strength is not to the point. If it is one of shifting large loads of bricks from point A to point B by hand, strength will be a great deal more to the point than great intelligence. Intelligence holds a special place because of the way in which exhibition of moral virtues requires thought, at least in the recognition that one's act is not unjust, but one can easily imagine situations in which strength would cease to be a virtue at all. As automation proceeds, there may eventually be no need for physical strength. Perhaps we ought to guard against emergencies and the breakdown of machines, but that does not show that strength is a virtue as long as the machines are working; it merely reminds us that prudence is a virtue in any circumstances.

Since the moral virtues are like that, they will be unchanging even though there might sometimes be appearances to the contrary. In our earlier discussion of the relationship between pain and cruelty we saw one way in which the vice of cruelty might seem to be open to change. One can imagine a world different from the one in which we live in that a number of desirable things can be produced only at the cost of pain. It might be that after suffering, and only after suffering, a man attained wisdom, ceased to be intolerant of the frailties of others, and could achieve greatness in any of a number of fields. To keep pain from somebody in such a situation would be to harm him; inflicting pain on somebody would not be cruel, but would be to do him a service. Cruelty in such a world would be wilfully saving somebody from pain. The relationship of cruelty to pain in that world is quite different from what it is in this one, and the list of cruel acts in that world will be quite different from the list of cruel acts in this one.

These facts, though, do not suffice to show that the vice of cruelty has changed in an important way, or that cruelty is a vice in one of the worlds but not in the other. The word 'cruel' does not simply name all those things that appear on the list of cruel acts in this world; it is a classification with a point, determining with reasons what goes on the list of cruel acts and what does not. What is cruel in this world is different from what is cruel in that world, but the things that are cruel in that world are cruel for just the same reasons as are the things that are cruel in this world. We simply have to examine the point of the notion of cruelty and the role that it plays in human life. What has changed is not so much the concept, or the vice, as the circumstances in which the concept is applied and the way in which the vice is exhibited. In circumstances in which I owe somebody money I can be unjust by not giving him money. In different circumstances, in which I do not owe him money, it need not be at all unjust for me not to give him money. We do not conclude that the virtue of justice has changed.

A similar point would apply if we found ourselves returned to a Hobbesian state of nature. It is not that cruelty would be a virtue in those circumstances; kindness remains a virtue and cruelty a vice in those conditions because the one makes a man apt and the other makes a man unapt for social life and departure from the state of nature. The circumstances there are so different from those with which we are familiar that an act which would be kind in our circumstances would be simply stupid in those. We ought to be kind in the state of nature, but we ought also to consider what kindness is and what makes it a virtue rather than considering simply a list of acts which are usually kind in the milieu in which we do act. We ought to be kind in the state of nature, but the call to be kind, there, is only *in foro interno*, not *in foro externo*. There is a question about whether it is possible to exercise the virtue of kindness in a war of each against all. In those circumstances, the quality of character that constitutes kindness cannot have the same point or significance as it is given by a co-operative situation, so a man who has that quality of character cannot exercise it with the same point or significance.

Not all virtues involve reciprocity. Justice does. Kindness, on the other hand, except insofar as it involves avoidance of injustice, does not. A man who helps another only on condition of or in hope of return does not exhibit the virtue of kindness. But to say that kindness, and the other virtues except for justice, do not involve reciprocity is quite different from saying that they do not require, in order to be effective, a background of security in the behaviour of others. To perform in the war of each against all an act that would be kind in this world would not be kind, but stupid. It would exhibit the vice of imprudence, one way of exceeding the mean that is kindness. The point of the concept of kindness, what makes it a virtue and leads us to classify as kind those acts and people that we do so classify, lies in a background of co-operation and not in one of the war of each against all. Kindness does not cease to be a virtue in the Hobbesian state of nature; it is simply that it is impossible to be kind there.

Chastity is not infrequently cited as something which used to be a virtue once, but is so no longer, now that methods of birth control have been improved, though the term does not seem to be applied in such cases to a quality of character. Industry is another example of what might seem to be a changing virtue: once it was an excellent thing for a man to be industrious, and only by industry could people live a comfortable life. As automation takes óver more and more of our work, it begins to look as though the social usefulness of industry might be less than that of an ability to pass one's leisure time happily and peaceably. Industry, it might seem, was once a virtue but has now been replaced by an ability to be lazy successfully.

In fact, it seems fairly clear that neither chastity nor industry was ever a moral virtue. Their morality comes out only when we consider them under broader headings. If the crucial point in the decline of chastity was the appearance of more effective contraceptives, then presumably the good thing about chastity was that it enabled one to avoid the trouble of having children for whom one could not or would not care. In those terms, chastity is not a moral virtue, but it would, in those circumstances and undertaken for those reasons, exhibit the virtue of prudence. Undertaken for other reasons, it might exhibit other virtues. In the same way and for the same sort of reason, industry is not a moral virtue but does, in the appropriate circumstances, exhibit other virtues such as prudence.

This explanation of the way in which virtues such as prudence can take on more particular forms in specific social contexts enables us to see how we might get a situation in which it appears that particular virtues can vary from one social grouping to another and from one time to another: differing circumstances from one time and place to another can mean that the general need the virtue meets will take on a different specific form. If the circumstances are such that chastity is prudent, and if those circumstances prevail for a reasonably long time, then the idea that chastity is virtuous may become so ingrained that it comes to be regarded as virtuous in itself, or simply as a virtue. Similarly, the idea that it is virtuous to be industrious might, in appropriate circumstances, become so much a part of the background against which people think that industry simply came to be regarded as a virtue in itself. Then, when circumstances changed, industry and chastity might cease to be virtues. This description in terms of their ceasing to be virtues is, I suppose, perfectly permissible, but one needs to be careful about what conclusions are drawn. To understand *why* being industrious or being chaste was a virtue then, as an instance in those circumstances of an unvarying virtue, is to see that no radical moral relativism follows.

The account of virtues that I have been setting out places great emphasis on co-operation and the sense of justice. Justice is, perhaps, the most ratiocinative of the virtues, and certainly the way in which co-operation and the sense of justice involve the working out of claims means that it might be difficult to include animals and even children within the realm of morality. To put the point crudely, animals and children are not fit to sign a social contract. My nastiness to my workmate may affect our co-operation, but my nastiness to a passing dog which plays no part in any human endeavour seems to have no effect at all on co-operation. Why, then, does it count as cruelty? It might well have effects on human beings: the dog's owner might be grossly offended, and the nice little old lady who happened to see me kick the dog might be so outraged as to have a seizure. The morality of offending people in that sort of way seems to be fairly clear, but what is at issue is the problem of cruelty to animals, not of cruelty to owners or passers-by. If kicking a dog is cruel to it, then one should not kick even unowned dogs in private. Since such beasts, unlike, perhaps, dolphins, are incapable of co-operation and a sense of justice, how can they take a place in the moral community at least to the extent that it is improper to treat them simply as objects? The problem does not arise, of course, if such beasts are capable of co-operation and a sense of justice. Since kindness and cruelty do not require reciprocity, the notion of being cruel to a dog or a snail does not raise the problems that being unjust to one would raise, but a similar problem does arise despite the fact that the animals cannot reciprocate, because the point of the other virtue concepts still lies in co-operation.

Kindness is not a virtue if it is calculated. It requires a certain immediate reaching out to help another, a certain lack of reflection or calculation. The man who does something, not simply because it will help another, but because he has worked out that he ought to do it, is not being kind, though he might exhibit another virtue such as conscientiousness. The man who does something, not simply because it will help another, but because by not helping the other in this case he will hinder himself in the long run, is not being kind but, depending on the circumstances, self-seeking or prudent. Kindness is not, as I have argued before, a consequentialist concept like *repair*, and the consequences that make that quality of character significant and worth marking off as a virtue are not themselves parts of the concept. Kindness is being willing to help others without requirement or expectation of return, and it is a good thing because it makes co-operation easier and more efficient. Kindness is not a willingness to help others *in order* to make co-operation easier and more efficient. Cruelty is a willingness to cause pain of one sort or another unnecessarily or just for the fun of it, and that quality of character is especially significant and worth marking off as a vice because it makes co-operation harder and less efficient. Cruelty is not a willingness to cause pain *in order* to make co-operation harder and less efficient.

Cruelty is a willingness to cause pain of one sort or another unnecessarily or just for the fun of it, and that particular propensity can be realised with any sentient creature, just as well with animals as with people. Exhibiting that quality of character in one's relations to an animal is being cruel to the animal.

The argument is not that somebody who takes great delight in causing pain to animals is more likely wantonly to cause pain to people, but simply that, whether the object of his attentions be an animal or a person, he is exhibiting a delight in causing pain. We all know the difference between a person and a housefly, and we have all been brought up to accord people special treatment. These lessons that we learn could become so ingrained that somebody might take the greatest joy in tearing the wings from houseflies and beating cart horses though it would never occur to him to be nasty to a person. How can his treatment of animals be cruel if he is so firmly drawing the distinction between animals and people? He does draw the distinction in his behaviour, but the quality of character that he exhibits is still the same one, cruelty, even though he exhibits it only in certain circumstances.

Perhaps a willingness to cause pain to animals has nothing in common with a willingness to cause pain to people, despite the apparent implausibility of that claim, but the unspoken assumption that what is at work in both cases is simply a delight in causing pain as such seems to be quite widespread, and it seems to me to underlie our ideas about cruelty to animals. It is very difficult really to imagine that the same quality of character does not underlie a delight in hurting animals and a delight in hurting people, as opposed to imagining a man who exercises the vice on animals but not on people. If the two tendencies really are quite separate, then perhaps there is no moral objection to hurting animals for fun.

We do assume that hurting animals for fun is nasty, but just as we assume that the two quantities of character are not separate.

The points that apply to cruelty to animals apply more obviously to cruelty to children. An infant not yet of the age of reason may not be capable of a full-blown sense of justice and hence not capable of meeting conditions of reciprocity, but he is undeniably a person. There is no possibility of driving in a wedge and showing that a desire to cause pain to children is quite distinct from and independent of a desire to cause pain to people. Children are special in that they are incipient adults, and they play parts as incipient adults in a number of social institutions, notably the family. A role in such practices carries rights and responsibilities which can be recognised as the child's because he is an incipient adult, even though he must, for the time being, be represented with respect to them by his parents. A child is an incipient adult who will eventually be able to exercise rights and fulfil responsibilities for himself, and it is because of that that he plays the role he does play in a number of our social practices. It is also because of that that a parent stands to his child in a quite different relationship from that in which an owner stands to his dog, and that it is possible to have strict obligations of justice to a child with his parent as agent. The practices impose those obligations.

The relation between brute animals and children or retarded adults is a real worry for moral philosophy, because there are many important ways in which the two groups are similar and some important ways in which animals are superior. For the first six months of life, a monkey is said to show more intelligence than a human being. Despite such facts, we give clear moral preference to people. It is not really obvious why we should do so.

Children and sufficiently retarded adults show no sense of justice or capacity to co-operate, so if that rules animals out of the moral community, it ought to rule out some people as well. There are, though, significant differences between the relevant people and animals. One fairly obvious one is that children are potential adults, and retarded adults look more like us than do Hereford bulls or even apes. That probably goes some way towards explaining why we do draw the distinction we draw, but it can also be used as the starting point for a possible argument to show that we are right so to draw the distinction. That we should have such sentimental regard for other beings similar to ourselves is a jolly good thing and at least helps to make life more pleasant. On the other hand, such sentimental regard does need to be limited. The death of a neighbour in a traffic accident is likely to upset us because it is near to home, but the death of somebody unknown in a traffice accident a thousand miles away will be ignored as boring and the death of hundreds in a Chinese earthquake will be passed off with a mere shudder. These reactions are not only common, but probably good. We might be able to comfort bereaved neighbours, but a feeling or show of concern will achieve nothing in the other cases. And we must have limits to these reactions: with the world as it is, if we were upset by every ordinary rape or mugging then we should all have nervous breakdowns and not get anything done. So, it might be said, we do concentrate on cases near to home, and it is good that we should do so. Children and retarded adults resemble us more than do giraffes or earthworms, so we do no wrong to concentrate on them.

This might serve as an explanation of why we react as we do, but it is obviously insufficient as a justification. The cat that sits by the fireplace, or the cow, part of which appears on the table, quite simply, are as near to home as children and retarded adults, and a lot nearer home than people caught in Chinese earthquakes. They are right there: we can kick the cat, and, if we cannot do much about the particular cow on the table, we can so act as to increase or decrease the market for its fellows and hence the likelihood of their being slaughtered. The fact that they look different from us simply is not enough when we can affect their fates so easily. It would be like ignoring a Chinaman caught in an earthquake in the house next door on the ground that all Chinamen look different and come from far away.

Children are potential adults, and might therefore quite reasonably be given roles in our co-operative enterprises with their rights exercised by adults as their agents. Retarded adults, even if they are not potential unretarded adults, are still different from brutes in an important way: they represent a possibility for us, not only for what we might have been, but for what we yet might become in case of unhappy accidents. It is, therefore, reasonable and prudent that they should be given roles with their rights exercised by other adults as their agents. They are not, so to speak, naturally in the community, but they are brought into it, and there is good reason why they should be brought in. The same prudence explains why they should be excluded from the community when there is not enough to go around. If there is simply not enough food to support all the people, then these are the people who have to go because they are the ones who have no rights of their own. One might even imagine cases, like the Dudley and Stephens case, in which it would arguably be right to eat them.

Nevertheless, in less than extreme circumstances, people who care at all about people will have a natural inclination to include children and retarded adults as being in the enterprise, and they should be encouraged to do so. That is part of the spin-off from the quality of character required for social life, even though the spin-off is not necessary to the quality of character.

EIGHT
Kindness

Kindness is not a matter of meeting obligations or doing one's duty. Obligations or duties, in general those things that can properly be required of us, are matters of justice. Because the grocer has a proper claim against me that I should pay my bill, I show no kindness in giving him the money required. In a clear sense, since he has a proper claim against me for that sum, what I do is to give him what is his rather than what is my own, and I can be kind only with what is mine. When I pay him I merely give him what is rightfully his, so that I do not place him under any obligation and I do not show any enormous moral merit in myself. I have done no more than meet his legitimate claims, and that is the least I can do. If legitimate claims cannot, by and large, be required and enforced, then social life would be impossible, and somebody who will do only what he can be forced to do is not kind.

This point, it should go without saying, does not hold good only in monetary affairs. I may owe the grocer money, but I can owe other people time, effort, patience, services of various sorts, and so on. If I am part of a baby-sitting circle, I may owe my neighbour two hours of baby-sitting time. That is probably quite readily translated into terms of money, if only because I could employ a baby-sitter to serve out my time, but the situation is not always like that. The convicted felon who owes a debt to society cannot pay it off by employing somebody else to serve out his time. If my neighbour was patient with me through a difficult period in which I went on a back-to-nature kick and insisted on keeping chickens in the city, then I owe him some patience when he starts to learn the violin. There is no obvious way in which that debt can be translated into terms of money.

Merely paying my debts is required of me by justice and does nothing to show that I am a kind man, but paying debts is not always a matter of merely paying debts. Circumstances that make a payment of debts other than routine may well enable us to show something about our character that would not be shown by, say, signing an order at the bank to have the rent paid monthly into the landlord's account. Paying debts might require fortitude or a very strong sense of justice if the circumstances are abnormal in a required way. Paying debts to the interior decorators who have just finished work on my shop may leave me without enough money to pay the protection racketeers, who will, as I well know, respond by smashing everything I own. That is not a routine payment of debts, and payment does not merely show that I have a routine sense of justice. Or it may be that I have all my life had a dream of spending a month writing poetry in a Parisian garret, and that a once-in-a-lifetime chance to do so comes up at a time when the only money I have I owe to my bookbinder in payment for journals he has bound for me. A fairly strong sense of justice, one perhaps worthy of special praise, might be shown by my overcoming temptation and paying the debt.

Along with other virtues, kindness can be shown in the paying of debts. One obvious way it might be shown is by paying a debt earlier than one need, but even payment at the last moment, or a bit late, can show kindness. I might pay a debt merely because I owe it, or because justice requires it of me, or there might be other reasons also working on me. If I owe money by a specific date, when I know I'll find it difficult to pay, and know that I could get away with not paying until it would be easier for me to do so, either because my creditor is a soft-hearted man or because it would take him a year to get a court order, I might, despite my weakened condition, take a second job and drive myself into ill health in order to earn the extra money needed to pay the debt in time. I might do it because I want my reputation as a regular payer of debts to stand up so that my bookbinder will continue to extend me credit; that might show prudence or an obsessive concern for the condition of my journals, but it does not show kindness. Or I might go to the trouble because I know that my creditor has a lifelong dream of spending a month writing poetry in a Parisian garret and now has a once-in-a-lifetime chance to do so which he can take only if the debt is paid on time. That does show kindness. I certainly owe him the money and do nothing which could not properly be required of me, and perhaps if that were not true I should not have gone to the same trouble in order to be able to loan or give him the money to take his chance. Nevertheless, that is not my only reason for giving him the money, and, if it were, I might well have made use of his soft heart and saved myself early decrepitude by taking longer over payment. I went to that trouble, not simply because I was or could be required to, but because of a desire to help him satisfy deep and long-felt wants, and that is kindness. I was not merely doing what was required of me, which can be done cold-heartedly, but was aiming at his happiness. In a similar way, one might be kind by refusing to pay a debt even when payment would be no trouble. That might happen if I risked a bad name by refusing to pay the debt because paying it would give my creditor enough money to invest in a fraudulent firm which would, in fact, make him lose everything he had.

What determines whether I display the virtue of kindness is not merely whether the act I performed could properly have been required of me, but whether that is the whole reason I did it. What matters is whether I was simply meeting requirements and would cheerfully have done no more than that, or whether, though knowingly meeting requirements, I was aiming at somebody else's happiness, which is not one of the things that could be required of me in the circumstances. I was aiming at his happiness for its own sake. Were I employed as some sort of attendant with the job of keeping somebody happy, I should show no kindness in aiming at his happiness if I did so simply because it was my job.

The claim that I can be kind only with what is mine is a significant one because it indicates an important limitation on kindness: in being kind I may give up or refuse to exercise my own rights, but I may not infringe the rights of others. Kindness is a virtue that can be established only within the limits of justice. Where a case of apparent kindness involves also a display of injustice, something has gone wrong.

There are cases which appear to go against this claim. A mother, for example, may, at least apparently, be kind to a sick neighbour by sending her son to cut the neighbour's lawn whether or not he wants to do it, and, though he is her son, she does not own him; she cannot, for example, sell his body to science. This, at least apparently, is a case in which somebody is being kind with somebody else's time and energy. There are at least two ways, though, in which we could see this as not a case of being kind with somebody else's effort, and in other cases we might well think that the mother was not being kind. One way in which we might regard this as not a case of being kind with somebody else's effort is by regarding it as what might be described as a case of unwilling kindness. The mother is bringing up her thirteen-year-old son; because of that, she has certain rights and responsibilities. In a variety of ways, she may and should act as his agent, and it is as his agent and partly with his good in mind that she makes her offer to the neighbour. She has her son's good in mind insofar as she sees her making of the offer on her son's behalf as something involved in bringing him up to behave properly, help others in need, and so on, and if that is part of her job then her offer is a proper one. She has genuinely shown kindness in recognising the neighbour's need and responding to it, though how much kindness she shows depends on whether she would have put her own effort into helping the neighbour had it not been that she felt constrained by her duty to bring her son up properly. But insofar as the effort is put in by the son and the offer is made by him through his agent and on his agent's decision, what we have is a case of unwilling, and therefore non-standard, kindness by the son.

Another sort of circumstance might equally explain how the mother is being kind with what is her own. The son lives in the family and has a place in the family, and the family is a small-scale co-operative endeavour. Because the son has a role in this co-operative endeavour he may well in fact, though it will not necessarily be so, owe his mother some effort. She might be able to claim payment of that debt from him in all sorts of ways, in washing up, raking leaves, or doing the shopping, and she properly shows kindness if she chooses to have the debt paid by sending her son, even against his will, to cut the neighbour's lawn. She is collecting a debt, that effort is owed to her, so she is not trying to be kind with what is not her own.

It should be borne in mind that not every case in which a woman sets out to be kind by directing somebody else to help another will actually be a case of kindness. A mother might have her timid forty-five year old son living with her and paying above-market prices for his board and lodging. If she sends him, against his will, to cut the sick neighbour's lawn because it is the right thing for him to do, she may be correct in her moral judgment, but she is being domineering and intruding on her son's life rather than being kind to her neighbour.

Another case in which one might appear to be kind with what belongs to somebody else would be a case in which one stole in order to give to somebody in need. For such a case to have any plausibility, it is probably necessary to add that one could not have provided what was needed from one's own store: a case, say, in which I am on a bare subsistence diet and steal in order to provide food for somebody who is starving. Were I a millionaire who stole in order to give alms to a beggar, there would be no inclination to say that I was kind; I merely intrude on the lives of others and keep all that is mine to myself. It is probably also necessary to add that the person from whom one stole could afford to give the required help to the needy person. Snatching one starving man's pittance to give it to another starving man does not show kindness; it shows lack of the imagination and judgment that are needed if one is to have any of the virtues. But if I, on a bare subsistence diet, steal from a millionaire (all of whose assets are in cash) in order to provide food for a starving man, and steal no more than is necessary to provide a bare sufficiency of food for him, then it might, with some plausibility, be claimed that I had been kind with what was not mine.

One way of dealing with this sort of case would be to say that what I gave to the needy person did not really belong to the person from whom I apparently stole it. It may have been his legally, but morally it was not; morally, he was required to give up that money, and there need have been nothing kind in his giving it up freely. What I took belonged to the needy person, not to the person from whom I took it, so I have used my efforts to help somebody by giving him what is his.

This sort of argument rests on the claim that there must be injustice in any society that allows one man to be a millionaire while another starves, and that at least part of that injustice is simply in that distribution of goods. This sort of claim is not an uncommon one; something like it lies behind a number of the justifications for sliding scales of taxation, and I think a version of it often does lie behind a lot of the attitudes that we commonly take towards cases of stealing from the rich to give to the poor. If the claim is correct, then the rich man has no just or proper claim on the money that is taken from him for the benefit of the poor, whether it be taken by taxation or by apparent theft; it was not properly *his* money, so in taking it I was not being kind with what belonged to somebody else.

An argument to sort out whether or not that principle was correct would be a very long and difficult one; it would involve both extremely delicate moral argument and a good deal of argument about the practicality and effect of various possible economic systems. I do not plan to argue the matter out; I merely note that the principle would give us one way of explaining why stealing from the rich to give to the poor is not being kind with what belongs to somebody else, and that acceptance of something like this principle seems to lie behind a lot of the attitudes taken to such activities by people who think that stealing from the rich to give to the poor is kind.

In some sorts of circumstances, as was said earlier, failing to show a virtue can itself amount to showing a vice. In some situations, simply failing to be kind, even though kindness cannot be required, amounts to being cruel or callous or unfeeling. The rich man who refuses to help when he would not even feel the loss of what somebody else needs is nasty; he is callous, and even giving something of which he would not feel the loss would not show him to be particularly kind. Perhaps we might think that such a man is so nasty as to deserve no better than to have some of his goods stolen for the benefit of others, but that is confused thinking that shows vindictiveness. If the goods cannot be required of him, and it is part of the story that, in the absence of the sort of redistributive argument we have just bypassed, they cannot be required of him, then taking them is simply theft and shows the vice of injustice.

But there is another reason why we might think that stealing to help the needy is kind, and is not a matter of being kind with what belongs to somebody else. I might be kind

insofar as I knowingly take the risks involved in theft for
somebody else, but not insofar as I am doling out somebody
else's goods. Taking risks for somebody else involves putting
a bit of myself on the line for his happiness; simply passing on
what belongs to somebody else does not. The same sort of
point holds if I help the needy person with money I need in
order to pay my debts to the grocer, and thus help him with
money that is, in an important sense, the grocer's. By stealing
or failing to pay debts I put myself at risk of trouble, so in each
case I am giving something of myself to help another. There is
sometimes a tendency to think of money I owe somebody else
or steal from somebody else as something I can buy or earn by
serving time in gaol or taking the risk of doing so. If we think
of the case in that way we shall not think of what I redistribute
as belonging to somebody else, so we can comfortably think
of it simply as kindness.

Another case that ought to be considered in this context is
one mentioned earlier: the case in which I refuse to pay a debt
(for the time being) because repayment would take my
creditor's assets to a sum large enough for him to invest in a
fraudulent company which will cost him all that he has. The
case is not intended to be one simply of differing financial
judgments in which I, assuming that I understand finance
better than he does, take it upon myself, like a guardian acting
on behalf of his ward, to prevent his making a bad investment.
It is intended to be a case in which he has been faced with
plausible arguments presented by plausible people in favour of
the company in which he now wants to invest. So plausible
were the people and the arguments that he will not believe my
report of a chance overhearing of a public house discussion
between the principals which made it clear that they planned
to fleece him. This is not simply a case of differing financial
judgments; I know something that he neither knows nor
believes, but I cannot prove it for want of corroboration.

It does not really seem clear here what the proper course of
action would be, or, in other terms, whether it would really be
kind to refuse to pay the debt at that time. If it is kind, then it is
an odd case of kindness: I should be kind to him by
withholding what is his, or kind to him at his own expense.
That one can be kind to somebody at his own expense seems a

strange idea. The right thing to do might be to pay the debt on time, report the overheard conversation, and leave it to him to decide whether to believe me and, either way, what to do about it. Or it might depend on other circumstances: if my creditor is also my friend, it might be my business (and to that extent not an unjust intrusion) to help him in that sort of way; in other circumstances it might be none of my business. But I want to examine briefly a couple of ways in which we might see refusal to pay as kind. There are a few points that might lead us in that direction for a start: in refusing to pay the money I owe I am aiming at somebody else's happiness rather than simply at the payment of any kind of debt, and nobody other than the person at whose happiness I aim (successfully, in the end) will be harmed except for the crooks, who will be harmed only in the pursuit of an illegitimate end. And I do risk something of mine, if only the acquiring of a bad name as a non-payer of debts.

One way of arguing that it would be kind to my creditor were I not to pay the debt would be to argue about what it is that I owe him. Do I owe him simply money, or something for his good? He loaned me money, and *prima facie* that was for my good; I needed it for something that I wanted, whether it be a new suit or payments to the protection gang who threatened all my new interior decoration. He did me a good turn, and now I owe him one. Normally, the good I owe him will take the specific form of money; I shall pay off my debt by paying him the money that he loaned me along with whatever interest was agreed on. This case, though, is different; I should harm him rather than help him by repayment of the monetary debt. What I owe him is a withholding of the money I owe him.

But this seems unconvincing in a number of ways. For a start, the talk of doing good turns, with its implications of the appropriateness of gratitude, sits ill if we talk of professional moneylenders who charge high interest and make a good living out of the activity. And the idea that what I owe my creditor is non-payment of the money is at least misleading. I have not paid the debt when I refuse to pay the money, though that is when I help him; I still owe him the money, and would show myself to be, not only unkind, but unjust if I refused to pay up when the danger had passed. The major remaining difficulty with the claim that what I owe him is a good turn, or something for his own good under that description, is that it suggests that the reason I ought to pay him is that it would be for his good, and that is plainly false. If that is the reason for giving him money, then whether or not I have a debt to him is completely irrelevant. Whether or not I ought to pay my debts is independent of my knowledge that a particular creditor will immediately head for Randwick and lose all that I have paid him plus more on the horses, or even by the knowledge that the inept fool will immediately sit down and lose what I paid him plus more in a poker game with me. In either case he will be worse off as a result of payment of the debt, but there is no doubt that I owe him the money and ought to pay up. If that is how he gets his kicks, then so be it. Being kind is indeed a sort of a mean, and one excess of it is sticking one's nose too much into other people's business.

There is another question that might be asked: if I pay him the money that I owe him in these circumstances, do I give him money or cost him money? When I pay him, I know that he is going to be financially worse off as a result; that may not be what I aim at in paying him, but I know that it will be one of the consequences of my doing so. It would be, in one terminology, a matter of indirect intention even if not a matter of direct intention. This point is not sufficient to explain why it might be kind to refuse to pay the debt, because it is a point that applies equally well when I know that he is going to waste the money on horses or poker, but it is part of the story. The rest of the story is that I know something that he does not, of which I am unable to persuade him, and that knowledge makes me more capable than he is himself of achieving his ends. If he chooses to lose his money on horses then that is his business, but he is not choosing to be defrauded; that is something he wants to avoid. If I refuse to pay the debt in this case, then, unlike the case in which I refuse to pay the debt because he will waste the money on gambling, which I think to be a bad thing, I am aiming at his ends rather than imposing my ends on him. Whether it would be kind to refuse to pay the debt, then, rather than paying it and ineffectively reporting the conversation that I overheard, depends on whether my extra piece of knowledge makes that particular sort of paternalism appropriate. That problem would need a lot of arguing out, and might depend on all sorts of circumstances. It might be appropriate in my relations with a friend but not in my relations with a professional moneylender. In any case, I do not simply refuse to pay the debt; I withhold payment temporarily, and must pay up when the danger has passed. Insofar as such paternalism is appropriate, I am not being unjust, and I am therefore not being kind with what is not my own.

Similar issues arise if it is a matter of my apparently being kind to aid somebody in committing injustice, as, for example, if I see that somebody wants money and so, out of a desire for his happiness, help him to rob a bank. Or, less impersonally, I might help him to snatch an old lady's purse. Once again, I am apparently being kind at the expense of somebody else. If the old lady will starve as a result of our ministrations, it might seem that I am kind to one person in a way that requires that I be cruel to somebody else. Is it possible to be kind in that sort of way? It is impossible to be just to one person in a way that requires that one be unjust to another (that cases sometimes seem to be of that sort merely shows that the justice of such situations is complicated). Because justice is a distributive concept, one is not so much just to a particular person as just between competing claims. Kindness is not like that; one can certainly be kind to a particular person. But can the display of one virtue, in particular cases, require the showing of other vices?

It might seem for a start that, say, courage could require imprudence, but that would depend on a misunderstanding of the virtues involved. Courage is not merely taking risks; it is roughly, taking risks in a worthwhile cause, and insofar as the case is worthwhile it is not imprudent to pursue it. If the cause is not sufficiently worthwhile to justify the risk, then pursuing it shows less courage than bad judgment. Judgment is important in the possession of any virtue. A person who is kind-hearted or well-meaning is not necessarily kind; if he lacks judgment, so that he consistently tries to do things that he is unable to do or consistently fails to recognise that some wishes expressed by people are merely momentary so that one should not try to satisfy them, he may mean well, but he is not kind. If he responds to the remark 'With pensions the way they are today, I'd give my right arm to be a cripple' by taking an axe to the speaker, he may have meant well, but he did not succeed in being kind. He was good-hearted, perhaps, and he may have acted for the best, but he was not kind. He was foolish. Without reasonable judgment, there is no virtue.

In some cases, we need knowledge. To be kind to the old lady who lives next door by fixing her leaky roof, I need to know how to fix a leaky roof. If a man crawls in from the desert croaking for water, it is not kind to give him a lot of water. I may mean well and be kind-hearted, but without the required knowledge I shall not succeed in being kind. The sort of judgment required, though, often takes a more complex form which can associate one virtue with others and which is itself associated with wisdom. A man who takes great risks to prevent his country's unjustly declaring war properly shows courage; he has taken risks for a worthwhile end, and the end is worthwhile morally. It might not have been worthwhile simply in terms of his own interests, since his country might have been strong enough to win the war easily and he, a seventy-three year-old blind man in a reserved occupation, might have been personally unaffected by the conduct of the war. A man who risks his life or a public riot to prevent somebody from spitting on the national flag does not show courage; that cause is not worth the risk, and the reason it is not worth the risk, again, is not simply a matter of his interests. Somebody's spitting on the flag will not affect his interests. Other virtues are being called on here in the judgment, and they are being called on in a way that might let us say simply that somebody who helps somebody else snatch an old lady's purse shows judgment sufficiently poor to rule out his being kind.

If one person should, in the sort of case described, set out with some sort of good will to help another snatch an old lady's purse, what could he have been aiming at? If his aim was to increase the general happiness, or to increase the happiness of the person he was helping because he thinks it a good thing if people are happy, then he shows remarkably bad judgment.

He is simply overlooking the effects his action will have on the old lady. Her loss and the felt invasion of her privacy will not increase the general happiness, and somebody who thinks that it is a good thing if people are happy could not with good will act towards her in that way. Perhaps he got so caught up with the interests of the person he helped that he never really considered the effects on the old lady, but the overlooking of the old lady, while it might have been done with the best will in the world, shows a lack of that sympathetic imagination required for good judgment.

Or it might be that he helped the thief because the thief was Fred, and he cared about Fred's happiness but not about that of the little old lady. He is still aiming at the happiness of another and risking a gaol term for himself in what he does in attempting to achieve that aim, and we do allow limits on the field in which anybody exercises his kindness: we cannot each of us be kind to everybody because there just is not the time. Attempts to be kind to everybody are, in the nature of the world we live in, bound to achieve nothing for anybody. The best we could aim at in practice would be to be kind towards all those we come across, and limitations on time, energy or financial resources might force us to limit the field further, giving first preference to our family, say, and spreading out from there. But the presupposition in those cases is that we do as much as we can and that we do not wilfully harm people outside the chosen group, and those presuppositions do not hold in the case of the man who helps Fred snatch purses. His concern is to see Fred do well at the expense of others, insofar as he aims at Fred's having everything he wants whether or not that conflicts with the wants of others, and that comparative, distributive notion raises issues of justice rather than of kindness. He is not kind, he is unjust.

The role of judgment in the exhibition of a virtue can show up in a variety of ways. Giving my all to no particular end is not kind, but silly. The father who risks his life by running into a burning house to save his infant son may show great virtue, but the father who risks his life to prevent his infant son's ears being sullied by the word 'Gosh' is simply a fool. A Jew who risked his life to save Hitler in 1940 would not be kind or courageous, unless he had reason to believe that Hitler would change his ways as a result, but imprudent and careless of the interests of other Jews. A man who, with some sort of good will, responds to the pleas of a drowning man by giving him all he has shows ignorance rather than kindness if all he has is an ancient collection of lead weights or a half share in I.C.I. Giving a robber a gun with which to hold me up is not kind; it is imprudent, and it is careless of the interests of others because the robber would then be in a better position to take advantage of them, too.

In a state of nature in which nobody co-operated with anybody else, it would be impossible to be kind. I have already argued that, from such a description of the state of nature, it follows with no further assumptions about human nature that everybody pursues his own interests single-mindedly because there is no way of resolving clashes of interests. (This does not mean that I must fight to the death for the turnip I found for my tea; my greater interest might lie in giving up the turnip as soon as somebody stronger demands it.) In such a situation, apparently being kind, helping somebody in a way not immediately in my interests (saving a drowning man, for example, for his good rather than because, in his weakened state, he represents a source of meat to me), is like giving a robber a gun with which to hold me up. It is, for a start, imprudent. It is helping somebody with whom I am in competition for survival, and giving my all for no worthwhile end. Since we are in competition for survival, the assumption must be that, in the long run at any rate, I give my life, but his life is worth no more than mine and there is no reason for the sacrifice. I have given my life to save a nasty fellow who is in competition with everybody else and will take their lives whenever it suits his interest and convenience to do so. I should be in much the same position as the Jew who saved Hitler in 1940. In helping to maintain a threat to other people in this way I am careless of the interests of others as well as careless of my own. So, in the state of nature, even if I set out to help, I fail to be kind.

We cannot be kind in a state of nature. The claim is not that we ought not to be kind, nor that it is not in our interests to be kind. Those questions do not arise, because it is *impossible* to be kind. The circumstances are not right.

Kindness takes its point from and requires a background of co-operation. It thus requires a context in which there is operating a sense of justice, and, without that, kindness is impossible. It is that point that rules out the possibility of our being, even in a state of civil society, kind and unjust in the same act. But, though kindness requires that background, it is not restricted to co-operation; I have already argued that kindness is not simply a matter of rights and duties, but of exhibiting a quality of character that can take on its significance only against that background. It is quite possible to be kind to passing strangers and budgerigars provided we are not in the state of nature.

Kindness is more than helping somebody; it is helping him for the sake of his happiness rather than for my own good. If the corner grocer does poor business and I take to giving him a large tip whenever I pay my bill because I am concerned for his welfare and that of his family, that is kindness. It is not kindness if I give him the tip to keep him in business simply because it is convenient for me to have a grocer nearby or because his being there puts pressure on a business competitor of mine. Nor is it kindness if I perform an apparently kind act but perform it for my own good in that it helps me to look respectable or to feel good about myself. (If performing moral acts is necessary to make me feel good about myself then I have some virtue, but it need not be kindness; it is more likely to be a species of conscientiousness.) One does not aim at being kind. If what I aim at is being kind rather than helping Bill, then I am concentrating on myself and whether I measure up to my standards or exhibit certain qualities of character rather than concentrating on Bill and his needs. Kindness is not a species of self-absorption. Consider those who perform apparently kind acts so that they can play some role in which they want to see themselves (martyr, devoted friend), or feel superior to those who receive their largesse, or so that they can feel needed; people for whom others provide an opportunity for a display to themselves. Consider those who force unwanted 'kindnesses' on others for that sort of reason. That sort of self-absorption and use of others rules out kindness. (Consider: how far can we trust them to continue to act in a kind way, and why? What is the quality of character that they exhibit?) Kindness is not self-conscious, as justice is. In order to be just, I must aim at being just; I must work out the correct relation between competing claims and be concerned that I do the right thing. That is why justice can seem a very cold and ratiocinative virtue. Being just involves being concerned with being just. But kindness is not self-conscious in that way; it does not require that one be concerned about being kind (in those terms), but that one be concerned about the happiness of another. Kindness is a matter of immediate warmth of feeling and care for others, exercised with good will and judgment.

NINE
Friendship

Being a friend is not simply a matter of having another social role to play. That I am no good as a carpenter may mean that I have chosen the wrong trade, but that I am no good as a friend entails that I have some moral failings. If I am postmaster, then my failing to get the mail out on time and, indeed, losing most of it, means that I am a bad postmaster; if I cheat and lie to John Smith, then I am not his friend at all. I cannot be a friend and fail at the relevant tasks as I can be a postmaster and fail at the relevant tasks, because friendship is not a matter of relevant tasks. Friendship is a notion the point of which is moral. It is to be understood, not as a set of jobs to be done, but as a relation considered in the light of a moral ideal.

Friendship is a matter of special relations. Friends are distinguished from acquaintances, strangers, and so on, partly by the fact that friends are people to whom we feel a lot closer than we do to most people. Our friends are not simply people whose company we enjoy, as we might enjoy simply standing in a group at a party listening to Fred tell more of his excruciatingly funny stories, and it is not enough to make the difference that Fred likes our company and seeks it out, too, because we are the only people who think his stories anything other than boring. Such facts might eventually lead to friendship, but they do not constitute friendship. Being somebody's friend is more than liking him and being liked. Friends are people for whom one will go further out of one's way than usual when they are in need of help, and they are the people to whom one is most likely to turn when one finds oneself in trouble. Friends are people who have a special trust in each other. That trust informs the sort of help that friends give to each other.

If a friend of mine has appendicitis, then he will not ask me to operate on him and I shall not offer to do so. When help of that sort is required, the person to turn to is a doctor. It might be argued that the special feature of that case is that, lacking the required knowledge and technical skills, I should be unable to help, so that the case reflects nothing about friendship, but that would be a misunderstanding. Friends do many sorts of things for each other, but they do those things in a special way. If I need help in building a greenhouse, I may seek and get that help from a friend, but his being a friend is accidental when he is helping me in that sort of way; anybody else could have given me that help. My neighbour might have helped me to build the greenhouse in return for my doing a repair job on his car or paying the complete cost of replacing our common fence. I should have received the same help, but it would not have been a matter of friendship. Friendship is not that sort of economic arrangement, which is why many people have a feeling of unease when entering into some economic arrangements with friends: friends are people for whom one is prepared to do something extra, and relations of buying and selling seem not to be like that. There is one well-established tradition that we go to a friend to buy a second-hand car because we get a better price that way, expecting the friend to cheat his employer or cut his own income in order to do us a service, though it might just as well be that, knowing nothing about cars, we go to him because we know we can trust him not to cheat us, and, perhaps, know him to be a fair man who will not cheat himself or his employer either. Friendship is compatible with economic arrangements, but is itself not a relation of that utilitarian sort and can sometimes sit ill with such arrangements.

My neighbour might help me build the greenhouse, not in order to get some service from me in return, but because he is a keen gardener or builder who cannot stand seeing a greenhouse botched up. That help is not an exhibition of friendship, either; friendship is not simply a matter of helping without expectation of service given in return. My neigh-bour's action in that case was not a matter of consideration for me, but of consideration for himself, or possibly the greenhouse. An act of friendship is done for one's friend, not for one's own gratification. And friendship is in some ways like an economic arrangement; it is not a matter of expecting return for this or that specific service or of keeping a set of accounts showing who owes what to whom, but it is a two-way relation.

It is not that, having had his help in building the greenhouse, I am now specifically bound to mow his lawn or anything of that sort, but, as he is in general prepared to help me because we are friends and has displayed that fact in particular by helping me to build the greenhouse, so I should in general be prepared to help him simply because we are friends. When friends help each other in this sort of way, they do not act in the expectation of immediate return, but they do act in a context making the assumption that help will be reciprocated when the occasion arises. This general reciprocity, or potential reciprocity, seems important to friendship, and is what makes it possible to recognise a friendship of utility as something distinct from a simple economic arrangement. One does not act with the expectation of specific return for specific service, but one does assume that the other will help when the help is necessary and he can provide it. This may be an empty assumption when the person one helps is himself helpless, perhaps an old friend who has been left paralysed by a car accident. The case would need to be a very strong one, though, if the person were to be incapable of building greenhouses, comforting one in times of depression, and trying to be entertaining. If somebody cannot perform physical tasks, or speak, or anything of the sort, it is by no means obvious that one could have friendship with him. Nor is it obvious that one can properly pass on without a qualm and abandon an old friend who finds himself in this position: friendship itself might require virtues which would lead one to remain and care for him in the new situation.

Because friendship is, in that way, a matter of reciprocity, it would not be an act of friendship if my neighbour helped me to build the greenhouse simply because he was a kind man and saw that I needed help. His act would not have been done in order to place me under an obligation to perform some service for him in return, and it would not have been done simply with the aim of satisfying himself, but it lacks the general context of friendly reciprocity; it is an act of charity rather than an act of friendship. If I am anything like a decent person then his act may lead to friendship, but his act is not one of friendship because the context of general reciprocity is not yet present. As far as friendship goes, what he did could be no more than an overture.

Acts of friendship, then, have a lot in common with acts of kindness, but they are performed in a special context. Part of that context, and a part which helps to mark off acts of friendship from such acts as giving alms to a beggar, is a sort of general reciprocity. So much emerges from the cases of friendship of utility that we have considered so far, but there is more to friendship than that. Friendship of utility is different from an economic arrangement, even a long-term economic arrangement in which we do not bother to keep accounts of who owes what to whom, in that it takes its colour from a different sort of friendship which is central to the concept.

The notion of reciprocity operating here is an odd one. We do not help our friends only after they have helped us, let alone help them only because they have helped us. Our helping them is not a matter of return for service; we help our friends because they are our friends and they need help, and the reciprocity in friendship is simply the fact that friendship is a two-way relation of that sort. Independently of what help my friend has given me, I shall help him when he needs it, and he will help me when I need it independently of what help I have given him. If my neighbour sits and laughs as I botch up my greenhouse that does not make him less of a neighbour, but if my friend simply sits and laughs then that does make him less of a friend. It might be that I need to be left to work on my own so that I shall not keep on expecting other people to do things for me, or leaving me to build the greenhouse on my own may be the best way to develop in me certain building skills, in which cases my friend might help me (though not in building the greenhouse) by simply sitting back and laughing, but, because he is my friend, he is supposed to help me when I need help and he can provide it. His less friendly neighbour might be building a greenhouse on the same day and might be even more inept than I am, but there is no particular reason why that should move my friend to help him rather than go swimming or sleep. The call on him to help me does not lie in the nature of building a greenhouse or in the simple fact that help is needed; it lies in the fact that we are friends, the same fact as might lead me to tell him to go swimming and leave the greenhouse to me. Behaving as a friend and acting for his good might mean not burdening him with my problems, and burdening him with my problems might show me not to be his friend. Nevertheless, the call on him to act lies in the fact that he is my friend and will act for my good. This remains so even though my friend's neighbour might be as virtuous and deserving as I.

Failing as a friend is a moral failure; being a friend is somehow related to the possession of virtues. Friendship is a phenomenon that has its place in the moral realm, and is something to be sought after rather than avoided. It might seem odd, then, that it involves partiality as we have seen it to do. My friend's virtuous neighbour, at least as deserving a man as I, is as much or more in need of help in building his greenhouse as I am in building mine, but my friend helps me simply because we are friends. My need of help is no greater than that of my friend's neighbour, and my virtue is no greater than his, so the display of friendship appears to be simple partiality, giving preference to me with no good moral ground for doing so. How can that sort of distinction drawn between people be proper? It has some of the surface signs of injustice. And how can friendship, which leads to and is expressed by the drawing of such distinctions, be a good thing? I have argued that justice is the primary virtue, but friendship seems to involve drawing distinctions not based on justice.

The drawing of distinctions not based on justice is sometimes unjust. A traffic policeman who hands out speeding tickets with a free hand but, simply out of love or fear, fails to give one to his wife, is behaving unjustly. And a judge who, because the accused was his friend, ignored the evidence and directed a finding of not guilty in a murder trial would manifestly have behaved unjustly, but there is all the difference in the world between hanging a man until he is dead and helping him to build a greenhouse.

Not all such distinctions are unjust. A mother who gives a slice of bread and jam to a neighbour's child does not thereby behave unjustly, but nor does she behave unjustly if she feeds only her own offspring and leaves the other children in the neighbourhood to the ministrations of their own parents. And a man who, faced with sixteen attractive women, invites only one of them to dine with him and does not base his choice on merit or virtue does not thereby display injustice; if he invited all sixteen of them he might display imprudence, at least in the form of fiscal irresponsibility.

So the drawing of distinctions not based on justice is sometimes unjust and sometimes not. To show that friendship requires injustice, we should have to produce more of a case than we have so far.

One might react to this so strongly as to say that special treatment of each other by friends is required by justice. Friends have closer ties with each other than they have with mere acquaintances or mere neighbours or mere colleagues; they do things together and for each other, and that sort of activity might well be expected to generate more claims between them than any of them would have with respect to other people who were merely acquaintances or something of the sort. If I have fixed his car and let him sleep at my house when his wife locked him out, then of course, it seems, he ought to help me with my greenhouse rather than help somebody who has done no more than move into the house next door and smile politely. We give precedence to our friends, and there is no injustice in doing so. Friendship generates extra claims because of the extra services that we render to each other.

This will not do, though; it depends on a misconstruction of the relation of friendship. If a profit and loss account had been kept, it might be that I was in debt to my friend at the time I set about building the greenhouse. If we have been keeping a profit and loss account, though, that suggests that we are not so much friends as people operating a rough and ready barter system. No reference to such an accounting system was necessary in setting up the case for my friend's helping me in building the greenhouse, because it is irrelevant. Friends help each other simply because they are friends, and that means that the one who would have been creditor had accounts been kept should be just as willing to help the one who would have been debtor as the other way around. The two-way relation in friendship is not a matter of return for particular services, but rather of a general willingness on the part of each to help the other.

If my friend's neighbour is a charming and attractive

woman, he may help her to build her greenhouse instead of helping me to build mine. That might even stop me from building my greenhouse; some of the heavier work might require two people if it is to be done at all, or my friend, with greater experience in that sort of work, might know how to perform certain sorts of task that I lack the knowledge to do. In that case, he might have let me down. He might, in a minor way, have failed as a friend. But if I should demand that he ceases this frivolity with his neighbour and help me, citing as reasons various services that I rendered him in the past, then I am failing as a friend. I am treating the friendship as a plain co-operative venture which each of us has entered only for his own good, turning the friendship into the sort of relationship that I have with my grocer. I cannot demand payment for goods and services rendered to a friend as my grocer can demand payment for goods and services rendered to me. The two are not comparable cases of obligation. The grocer serves me in order to earn payment, and when I accept his service I place myself under an obligation to pay. It is a genuine obligation; he can properly insist that I meet it. When I help my friend, I do so, not in order to earn payment, but in order to help him. He may later do things for me in recognition of my service, but for me to demand payment for the act shows that what was offered under the guise of friendship was not really friendship at all. Receiving help from a friend is not like receiving payment of a debt. The relation between creditor and debtor ends with settlement of the debt, and the people concerned might reasonably part and never think of each other again. Friends do not so part when each has helped the other.

Relations between friends are, indeed, closer than relations between acquaintances or colleagues, and those closer relations might generate special ties (though they might be the sorts of ties that are expressed, rather than generated, by the close relations). Even if those special ties are generated, they are not the sort of tie that an ordinary case of obligation is. One friend might feel a tie that would lead him to help another, but the other cannot demand that of the first. To say that justice requires (rather than allows or forbids) preferential treatment for one's friends is too strong.

There are various sorts of ways in which we can give

preference to some people over others. Some of these ways are objectionable while others are not. In rough terms, the examples we considered earlier suggest that the drawing of distinctions not based on justice is unjust if it involves a dereliction from duty or an infringement of rights, but otherwise is just. The traffic policeman and the judge have a duty to apply laws impartially; they fail to carry out that duty if, in applying the laws, they discriminate between people in terms of whether they like them or not. A mother may have a duty to feed her own children, but she has no duty to feed or, usually, not to feed other children. Nobody, in the normal run of things, has a duty to invite any woman out for dinner. If we do not infringe rights or fail to carry out a duty, we do no injustice. If we discriminate between people and give preference to some over others, no injustice is done if we do not infringe rights or fail to carry out duties. And no injustice is done if we voluntarily give up our own rights.

So, even though friendship involves giving preference to people simply because they are friends, it need not involve injustice. Friends might be expected to give preference to each other in matters which infringed nobody's rights, or they might be expected to sacrifice themselves for each other. This would still allow friendship to have the place it has in the moral sphere, but it would severely limit the sort of help for which friends could look to each other: it means, for example, that we could not look to a friend on the draft board to help us being conscripted into the army, or to help us avoid detection and payment of damages when we have broken somebody's window or smashed into his car. It means that we could not turn to friends to hide us from the police when we have committed a crime. This would be a distortion or corruption of friendship, acting so as to corrupt a friend and perhaps even put him in danger rather than acting for his good. And yet criminals surely would turn to their criminal friends when on the run from the police. Aren't friends supposed to stick together through thick and thin and help each other in time of trouble? And yet, if friendship is a good thing, how could it have results such as those?

Perhaps, in some sense, a perfect world would be a world in which everybody was the friend of everybody else. It certainly does not follow that this world is like that, and it does not follow that it is appropriate to behave in this world as it would be appropriate to behave in that one or that, by doing so, we are most likely to bring that perfect world about. In a perfect world my baseball team might win all its games, but to bat in the top of the ninth in the manner appropriate, to a team that has a clearly won game, is not to bat in the manner appropriate to the circumstances in which my team usually goes into the ninth, and would not be likely to give us a win. In this world, perhaps friendships ought to be kept up even though they do involve preferential treatment, and perhaps friendship could be a good thing even if it had some bad consequences such as the hiding of criminals from the police.

In a perfect world, everybody might be the friend of everybody else, but it does not follow even that this world could be like that. In fact, it seems to be a practical impossibility. There is an enormous number of people in the world, and it is a practical impossibility that anybody should know them all to the extent of simply knowing their names. Spending time in people's company with reasonable frequency may not be a necessary condition of friendship with them, but it helps. Some sort of communication with them at some stage is a necessary condition, and there simply is not time for us to see everybody or write to them. Practical matters of that sort are sufficient to rule out the possibility of everybody's being a friend of everybody else.

Friends sympathise with and feel for each other. This feeling is an important part of friendship and is why we do things for each other simply because we are friends; the feeling or sympathy involved in friendship motivates and explains the actions. We commonly grieve if a friend suffers or dies; we rejoice if a friend does well. The world at any given time contains apparently innumerable cases of suffering, death, and causes for rejoicing; to be friends with everybody and react to all these cases at once would simply drive us insane. The alternative is to feel instead a fairly cool regard for others, to do what we can for them when they are suffering and to offer quiet congratulations, if it is not inconvenient to do so, when they do well, but in neither sort of case to feel at all upset about it.

Surely this is the minimal sort of behaviour that we owe to everybody, not merely to our friends, but equally surely it falls short of friendship. It might somehow be nice if everybody were the friend of everybody else, but it is impossible that that should be so. Friendships might give preferential treatment to some over others, and they might sometimes lead to the perpetration of injustices such as the hiding of a criminal friend from the police, but friendship could still be a good thing because it was an exhibition, even if only a partial exhibition, of willingness to co-operate in the form of the sympathetic bond between friends.

As people are and as the world is, discouraging that partial exhibition might discourage the whole social instinct. The partial exhibition, though imperfect, might be the best that we can, in fact, have; if it is, that would explain why friendship is a good thing and has the place it has in the moral realm. The friendship that leads us to hide a criminal from the police would then be seen as related to a virtue as is the state of character that exceeds courage to be foolhardiness. Friendship is not itself a virtue, and, on the account being canvassed, it would be seen as the imperfect setting in which we develop and imperfectly display other virtues; a setting which, though imperfect, is better than any other available. In this sort of way it might be possible satisfactorily to account for the morality of friendship even if it does involve some inclination towards injustice, and because of the way in which the account requires recognition that this is an imperfect world, it would not contradict my thesis about the role of justice in morality.

One should distinguish different sorts of cases when it comes to hiding criminals from police. If a friend committed a minor crime, then we might refrain from turning him in to the police because we thought he had got a big enought fright to learn his lesson, we knew him well enough to be sure that he would reform, and he would be ruined by any police proceedings or publicity. We should then be acting for his good, not seeking to corrupt him, and we might take the same line with minor criminals who were not friends of ours. It is not clear that any injustice would be done. But when it comes to hiding professional hit-men, then we have a corruption or distortion of friendship.

It is often pointed out that we are less upset by a plane crash that kills a hundred Chinese in China than we are by a car crash killing one person outside our front door or even by our six-month-old baby's breaking his arm. The claim is surely correct, and there are good reasons why it should be. We cannot get upset about everything unfortunate that happens, or we should be incapable of doing anything about a few things that happen. We cannot usually do very much about plane crashes in China, anyway, and where we can do something, such as sending blankets or food after a flood or hurricane in some distant place, we do expect people to react. A propensity not to feel too upset about distant disasters in which we cannot help will probably leave us more able to act effectively in situations nearer home on which we can have some effect — we can call an ambulance, at least, if there is a crash outside our front door, and we had better take the baby to hospital if he has broken his arm.

A tendency to feel less about distant major disasters than about lesser unfortunate events nearer to hand might be a good thing as the world stands, and I have been trying to show that the same point could hold true of friendship and special care for other people. This partiality may be a limitation of human nature, but, given the way the world actually works, it is a misconstruction to regard it simply as a fault. It may sometimes have ill consequences, but it is nevertheless the best that we can do. None of this means, as should be clear from what I have said, that it is proper for us simply to ignore or be cruel to those outside our own group. We cannot feel for everybody and we cannot help everybody, but we should avoid harming people whenever we can. We should avoid wherever possible inflicting on others the consequences of the world's and our own imperfections.

That is one way in which we might deal with the problem of friendship's being a good thing (the best of that sort that we can have in this world) even though it sometimes leads friends to favour each other unjustly. It is an imperfect world, and these are imperfect friendships falling short of the ideal. More needs to be said about it, though, and about why such friendships must be regarded as imperfect. There is something drastically wrong with a friendship that leads one man to favour another to the extent of protecting him from the police while an innocent man is left to hang.

Friends do a wide variety of sorts of things for each other, but there is a range of things done specifically by friends. These things involve trust. What marks off one's friends is not so much the kind of help that one is prepared to give them as the kind of help that one might be prepared to accept from them — help which could be given only if they knew things about us that we should not want to be generally known. We trust them with that sort of knowledge about our private lives, financial affairs or whatever.

Again, more needs to be said than that we trust our friends, because we trust other people as well. Our being prepared to walk city pavements implies that we trust drivers to keep to the road, but we must also trust people other than friends with the sort of information we should not want to be spread about. If my problem is enuresis, I may confide in a doctor or even in a behaviourist psychologist. I should be embarrassed to have people at large, including most of my friends, know of the problem, but I trust the doctor to keep the information confidential. That does not make the doctor my friend. One reason I trust him is that I know it would be worth his lucrative practice were he to divulge his patients' secrets, and that is not the sort of reason for which one trusts a friend. It goes with the fact that there is a strict limit on the sort of thing I am prepared to tell the doctor: I may tell him about the enuresis, but any worries about my financial affairs and whether I shall be able to pay his fee I may well keep to myself. That is not a matter within his field of professional competence, and I am consulting him in his capacity as a doctor.

But it is not always professionals that we seek out or special advice that we are looking for. Sometimes we do not want advice at all; we simply want to talk about our troubles, either because that just makes us feel better by itself, or because it helps us to sort them out. In those cases we may not go to our friends, and may deliberately avoid inflicting our problems on them. In that sort of case, a stranger will do just as well. And a real stranger can be trusted. Somebody I meet on the train and will never see again is a person for me to talk to, but, in a very important way, he is not a person in my world; he may pass on my innermost secrets to everybody he knows, but the story will not be passing around amongst my acquaintances. And because I shall have no further dealings with him, he cannot use my secrets against me. The worst he can do is dine out on stories beginning 'I met this weird fellow on the train . . .', which will not harm me at all. I can trust him in the way that I do because I have these external guarantees that my talk will not hurt me. That does not make us friends even if he unburdens his soul to me as well. Trust between friends requires no such external guarantees.

Sometimes I may be able to trust somebody because I have some sort of blackmailing hold over him or am behind him all the way with a gun. Again, this sort of external guarantee is what gives rise to the trust, and it is not a case of friendship because, though we can somehow trust each other, we cannot do so for the right reasons.

Or one person might trust another because he knows him well and knows him to be a decent person. Such a person not only likes or loves the other, but respects him. His trust is not simply based on the other's current emotional state, but on his settled character. That is the trust appropriate to friendship, which marks it off. I do not trust my friends to be kind and fair to me because they like me, but because they are kind and fair. I trust them because they deserve trust. No doubt we have interests in common which lead us to spend time together, be the common interest in canoeing, economic theory, or the improvement of race relations. Friends do not merely sit around respecting and admiring each other, and there must be something to draw them together in the first place, but friendship goes beyond the mere sharing of interests. Friends are not replaceable by somebody else with the same interests, as acquaintances, by and large, are. The common interests draw us together and help us to spend time pleasantly in each other's company, but it is the trust that makes us friends.

The role of trust in friendship explains the moral dimensions of that relationship. That I lie and cheat, am unjust and disloyal, gives nobody any reason to trust me. Being trustworthy involves having certain virtues; one is fit or unfit to be a friend as one has or lacks those virtues. One need not simply have or lack any given virtue but may have it to some degree, as some kind people are kinder than other kind people, and one might have some virtues but lack others, or perhaps have them in differing degrees. Friendship, plainly, is not something that one simply has or lacks. The degree to which one is fit to be a friend depends on the degree to which one has or lacks the appropriate virtues, and friendships can be better or worse depending on the degree to which the people involved are fit to be friends. And having a virtue to some degree need not be a matter of being, say, sufficiently kind to give a beggar one dollar but not to give him two; one might exhibit a virtue by and large, but be weak when faced with certain sorts of temptation. One needs to know that sort of thing about one's friends in order to avoid putting the friendship under unnecessary strain. Intimacy is required for a real appreciation of the stresses under which somebody acts, any odd beliefs he may hold, and so on, and that sort of knowledge is necessary if we are to be able to see whether and to what extent somebody exhibits a virtue and, therefore, the extent to which he can properly be trusted. This intimacy is presupposed by trust and admits of degrees, so friendship itself, no matter how fit each party may be to be a good friend, admits of degrees. The moral ideal gives point to friendship, but friendships admit of degrees and may be imperfect.

Once we see friendship in this way, something can be done towards expaining the friendship between criminals who hide each other from the police to protect each other from the consequences of their acts. As we have already seen, the man who feels an obligation to do his bit and help the gang to rob banks has a warped sense of justice. It is recognisable as a sense of justice because it shares formal elements with a proper sense of justice; if the world were somehow confined to the gang, he would be displaying a proper sense of justice. It is recognisable as warped because he fails to realise that the sort of relationship operating within the gang to produce the apparent obligation also operates between members of the gang and other people in ways that override the apparent obligations within the gang. Similarly, their friendship is recognisable as friendship but is warped and involves the exhibition of warped virtues. We can recognise it as a sort of model of friendship, but friendship gone wrong. Their possession of the appropriate virtues is minimal.

Friendship requires virtues, and acts of friendship display virtues. Being a friend involves, to a very large extent, doing the right or proper thing, so being a friend requires that one retain one's independence of viewpoint. Becoming so absorbed in another that one loses independence of viewpoint and simply acts to please is a move away from friendship towards something which is both more transitory and less worthwhile, even if it is sometimes more exciting. Best friends are the people we look to for unpleasant information about ourselves; we should be able to trust them to be accurate, not to act simply so as to hurt, and to act for our good rather than simply as toadies who will tell us only what we want to hear. We should also be able to trust them to respect our independence as part of our good, so that they will not constantly be offering unsought advice or acting paternalistically so as to achieve our good even if it be against our wishes.

The virtues displayed especially between friends will be more particularly the supererogatory virtues, so that any preference one friend gives another will involve no injustice to any third parties. Friendship requires and displays virtues. Possession of virtues is something that admits of degrees, but if one has virtues in any degree one has them, one does not have them simply for one's friends. A kind man is not kind to those he likes and cruel to the rest; a man whose actions depend so strongly on his passing feelings is too fickle to be trusted very far. One may be more inclined to be more kind to one's friends that to others similarly situated, just as one may be more upset by a car crash on the street outside than by a plane crash in China, but kindness does not simply restrict itself to a specific group or depend on whom one likes. Lying to or cheating anybody tends to show that one is not fit to be a friend, and one point distinguishing friendship from carpentry is that to the extent to which one is not fit to be a friend one is not a friend. The notion of friendship has built into it these safeguards against the giving of too much or improper preference to one's friends. If my friend's attractive neighbour is needier than I, he might show himself less fit to be a friend if he did not help her build her greenhouse rather than help me build mine, though he might show himself to be a less useful acquaintance if he did help her.

The virtue that leaps to mind as most strongly connected with friendship is the virtue of loyalty, though this virtue is at least equally, and perhaps more, at home with organisations and groups of people not especially involving friendship. One may be loyal to the elected government, for example, or a traitor to one's class. Loyalty is an odd virtue. Compare it with fortitude: neither is a virtue that could exist on its own. Courage might be marked off as a specifically military virtue, perhaps, but fortitude, as the willingness to stand up against danger for what is right, is a part of every virtue. The man who is just or kind or prudent only when it is easy to be so has those virtues at best minimally. Being just when it involves effort or risk is part of what being just is. Fortitude is, in that way, part of the virtue of justice, separable from the rest insofar as we can recognise that somebody wants to be just but is, say, easily frightened. Loyalty, as faithfulness to obligations, can be seen as a species of fortitude; it is sticking to the group and recognising the group's claims even in the face of danger or other temptation. Fortitude, and its specific form of loyalty, are strongly dependent on the other virtues through which they are exhibited. As we can see a warped sense of justice in a criminal organisation, so we can see a warped idea of loyalty there, too. So loyalty is not the recognition of excessive or improper claims by one person in a way that infringes the proper claim of another; that would be at best misguided loyalty, and one would suspect that it might be less loyalty than a concern for one's acceptance by the group. That is quite a different thing; a concern about oneself is by no means the same as a concern about the proper claim of others. Loyalty, as bound by the other virtues through which it is expressed, will not make friendship lead one to give improper preference to one's friends.

Concluding note

My main purpose in this book has been to argue that moral reasoning is basically a matter of reasoning in terms of virtues and vices and that it holds a quite special place in reasoning in general. Reasons of justice necessarily provide compelling reasons for action and reasons concerned with the other virtues necessarily provide good reason for acting, so a person has reason to be moral if he has reason to do anything.

What follows from my argument is not that a person who is immoral contradicts himself, nor that he is arbitrary, unintelligent, or incapable of reasoning. What follows is that he acts for bad reasons or is unreasonable, and it follows from the structure of reason itself forced on us by the conditions of human life. Human life is, at its base, unavoidably co-operative, and it is possible only if people for the most part have the qualities of character necessary for co-operation. They must have and encourage a sense of justice, and it is desirable that they have, and no accident that they encourage, the other virtues.

The claim I make is not that everything is just, nor that everybody or anybody believes that everything is just. It is, rather, that people must have a sense of justice and an inclination to accept reasons of justice as reasons for acting. People may hold strange and false beliefs which affect their judgment of what is just. They may make mistakes in their calculations. They may be weak-willed. But they must, by and large, operate with a sense of justice. And for similar reasons they must, be and large, encourage the development of the other virtues.

The arguments in this book are limited in their scope; they are bare, and they leave a lot of loose ends. Covering the bare patches and following up the loose ends is not a job for philosophers alone. Work in sociobiology may help add flesh to the skeleton set out here. It may help in sorting out what qualities of character are virtues, and one of its primary concerns might be construed as that of explaining the development and transmission of those qualities of character from generation to generation.

Work by psychologists on moral development, factors affecting sympathy with others, interplay between people in co-operative relations, and the formation of the sorts of attitudes involved in possession of the various virtues would all be to the point. The work I have done here, if it is sound, might suggest some lines of enquiry in those areas.

And my arguments do require further philosophical analysis of such problems as whether virtues can properly be accounted for as dispositions, the relation between possession of a virtue and performance of an action exhibiting that virtue, and so on.

It would be too much to hope that I have settled anything. It would be enough if I have opened a can of worms.

Index